KINGDOM,

COME!

Select List of Other Crossway Books by Phil Ryken

Grace Transforming

Christian Worldview: A Student's Guide

Loving the Way Jesus Loves

King Solomon: The Temptations of Money, Power, and Sex

Justification

Is Jesus the Only Way?

Our Triune God: Living in the Love of the Three-in-One (co-author)

KINGDOM,

COME!

PHIL RYKEN

WHEATON, ILLINOIS

Kingdom, Come!

Copyright © 2013 by Philip Graham Ryken

Published by Crossway
        1300 Crescent Street
        Wheaton, Illinois 60187

TELL OUT, MY SOUL
Words: Timothy Dudley-Smith
© 1962, ren. 1990 Hope Publishing Company, Carol Stream, IL 60188.
All rights reserved. Used by permission.

Cover design: Erik Maldre

Cover image: Makoto Fujimura
Zero Summer
2003–2004
Mineral Pigments on Kumohada
89 × 66 in. (226 × 167.6 cm)
© Makoto Fujimura

First printing 2013

Printed in the United States of America

Trade paperback ISBN: 978-1-4335-3404-1
PDF ISBN: 978-1-4335-3405-8
Mobipocket ISBN: 978-1-4335-3406-5
ePub ISBN: 978-1-4335-3407-2

Library of Congress Cataloging-in-Publication Data

Ryken, Philip Graham, 1966–
   Kingdom, come! / Phil Ryken.
      pages cm
   Includes bibliographical references and index.
   ISBN 978-1-4335-3404-1
   1. Second Advent—Sermons. 2. Sermons, American—21st century. I. Title.
BT886.3.R95   2013
236'.9—dc23   2013000563

Crossway is a publishing ministry of Good News Publishers.

To the alumni of Wheaton College
who work for the kingdom
and live in hope for the coming of the King.

Contents

Preface

One of the many privileges of my calling as a college president is to travel around the country and tell people what God is doing at my school, Wheaton College.

At one of our alumni gatherings, someone asked me whether I thought evangelical pastors were still preaching as often as they once did about the second coming of Jesus Christ. I had to confess that I didn't think they were preaching about that very much anymore. In fact, I couldn't remember any sermons focusing on eschatology from our previous year of chapel services.

Not long afterward I decided to take the coming of Christ and his kingdom as the theme for my chapel addresses during the following academic year. Those messages—which were first preached in 2011–2012—have now been edited to form the chapters in this book.

Here I need to express my thanks to Lydia Brownback, Tara Davis, Lynn Wartsbaugh, and Marilee Melvin for helping produce this book. Even more, I need to acknowledge my gratitude to God for everyone who prays that my ministry will be a blessing on our campus, and beyond.

"Kingdom, Come!" is the hope of every weary believer who waits for this tired world to come to its consummation. It is the desire of every longing disciple who hungers to see everything made new. It is the expectation of every faithful Christian who longs to see Jesus face to face. And it is the prayer of my heart as I finish this preface—as I hope it will be your prayer when you read this book: "Come, Lord Jesus!"

1

The Kingdom Is Near

Suddenly they began to appear all over the country: billboards announcing the end of the world. "HE IS COMING AGAIN!" some of them read, followed by a specific date on the Gregorian calendar: May 21, 2011. "SAVE THE DATE!" others proclaimed. "RETURN OF CHRIST. May 21, 2011." Then there were the billboards that sounded an alarm: "Blow the trumpet . . . warn the people. Judgment Day May 21, 2011. THE BIBLE GUARANTEES IT." On some billboards the number 2012 was printed down in the corner, circled in red and then crossed out, to indicate that the year 2012 would never arrive.

These billboards supported the radio teaching of one of America's most famous false prophets, Harold Camping. Mr. Camping first predicted the end of the world for May 21, 1988, and then again for September 7, 1994. Later he predicted that on May 21, 2011, judgment would come, Christ would return, the righteous would be raptured to heaven, and the world would be visited with five months of fire and brimstone.

Not Soon Enough

All of these prophecies turned out to be good for the beleaguered billboard industry. Starting on May 22, a new set of billboards appeared in response to Mr. Camping and his false prophecy. "That was awkward," they said, and then they provided a relevant text from Scripture: "'No one knows the day or the hour . . .' Matthew 24:36." Undaunted, some of Mr. Camping's followers remained convinced that they knew when the end would come. May 21 was only a spiritual judgment, they said, but the universe would be destroyed the following autumn. Their billboards now listed May 21, 2011, as the date of "The Rapture" (in a spiritual sense) and October 21, 2011, as "The End of the World." But these prophecies, too, turned out to be false.

In considering Mr. Camping's followers, it is hard to know whether to laugh or to cry. Looking to make a fast buck, some enterprising atheists from California advertised a post-rapture pet-sitting service and took nonrefundable deposits from animal lovers who wanted someone to look after the pets that would get "left behind" if suddenly their owners disappeared because they were taken to heaven.[1] More tragically, some radio listeners quit their jobs, spent their life's savings, and emptied their children's college accounts to warn people about the coming judgment, getting the word out over the radio waves and on highway billboards.

Christians who knew their Bibles criticized the preacher for being too specific. They rightly pointed out that when Jesus taught his disciples about the coming judgment, he told them that "concerning that day and hour no one knows, not even the angels of heaven, nor the Son, but the Father only" (Matt. 24:36). Therefore, anyone who presumes to predict the day the world will end speaks in direct contradiction to the true words of Jesus Christ.

These criticisms were valid; Mr. Camping was being much too specific. But there is another problem with predicting the day when the world will end: such prophecies push our expectation of the return of Christ and the coming of his kingdom too far out into the future. The problem with saying that Jesus will come again next October is not that he probably won't come that month after all, but that we should expect his return much sooner! The Bible's last prayer ought to be our daily expectation: "Come, Lord Jesus!" So we pray the way Jesus taught us to pray, "Your kingdom come" (Matt. 6:10).

The world may scoff at our hope in the second coming and at our belief in the imminent return of Jesus Christ. In fact, when a group called American Atheists invited the general public to a "Rapture Party" in San Francisco for the day after May 21, 2011, their billboard said, "2000 Years of 'Any Day Now': You KNOW it's Nonsense." Admittedly, there is usually a lot more nonsense in what Christians believe about the end times than there ought to be. Nevertheless, the Bible teaches us to live in hope for the coming of Christ. His kingdom is near.

The Coming of the King

We know that the kingdom is near because Jesus said it repeatedly. From the very beginning of his public ministry, he announced the coming of the kingdom of God. We see this clearly in the Gospel of Mark, which begins with words from Isaiah, Malachi, John the Baptist, and then from God the Father himself, declaring Jesus to be his "beloved Son." But what would Jesus say, when he finally spoke? Mark tells us that he came "proclaiming the gospel of God, and saying, 'The time is fulfilled, and the kingdom of God is at hand; repent and believe in the gospel'" (Mark 1:14–15).

People say you never get a second chance to make a first impression. Jesus had been waiting for this moment all his life. He had thirty years to prepare his opening line.[2] And this was it: "The kingdom is near." Of all the things Jesus could have said, of all the ways he could have preached the good news and described the plan of salvation, he started with the coming of the kingdom of God. As the gospel begins, the Son of God strides onto the stage of human history to make the eschatological announcement that his kingdom is at hand.

The coming of the kingdom may not be a very prominent theme in the church today, but it was central to the teaching ministry of Jesus Christ. The reason for this, of course, is that Jesus is the King. So when he comes, the kingdom comes. Here is how Christoph Schwobel explains it: "The imminent coming of the kingdom of God is a center of Jesus' message, and when he is confessed as the Messiah, the Son of the living God, the coming of the kingdom of God is so closely related to his person that he is in his person seen as the coming of the kingdom of God."[3]

Our Once and Future King

If this is true—if the coming of the kingdom is closely related to the person of Christ as king—then this explains why the kingdom is still at hand. There is a sense in which the kingdom has already come. It came when Jesus came, exactly as he announced. But there is another sense in which the kingdom is still to come. The kingdom is coming because Jesus is coming again, to reign in the full supremacy of his risen majesty.

A good, simple definition of the kingdom of God comes from Graeme Goldsworthy, who says it is "God's people in God's place under God's rule."[4] God does not establish his rule in all places all at once. In fact, Jesus emphasized this in some of his parables—the slow advance of the kingdom of God. The kingdom of God is like yeast, he said, that gradually works its way through the dough, or like a little mustard seed that eventually grows to become a tall tree (Luke 13:18–21).

So we live in kingdom tension—the tension between

the inauguration and the consummation of the kingdom of God. The kingdom has come in the person of Jesus Christ, who said, "The kingdom of God has come upon you" (Luke 11:20). As we submit to his lordship and surrender to his sovereignty, we are living the kingdom life. Wherever we live and worship, work and play, is a place where the kingdom has come (at least insofar as we actually live for Christ our King, submitting to his rule for our lives, even in the little things). James Davison Hunter comments: "As Christians acknowledge the rule of God in all aspects of their lives, their engagement with the world proclaims the shalom to come. Such work may not bring about the kingdom, but it is an embodiment of the values of the coming kingdom and is, thus, a foretaste of the coming kingdom."[5]

The Bible constantly reminds us that the kingdom is not yet here in all its fullness, and to that extent it is still coming. This hopeful expectation runs right through the New Testament. We see it in Paul, who said, "Our citizenship is in heaven. And we eagerly await a Savior from there, the Lord Jesus Christ" (Phil. 3:20 NIV). We see it in Peter: "Set your hope fully on the grace that will be brought to you at the revelation of Jesus Christ" (1 Pet. 1:13). And of course we see it in the Revelation of John, with all its prophecies of kingdom come. The King has come, and he is coming again. His kingdom is both here, and not here.

Frankly, Christians haven't always handled this tension very well. There is something about the imminent return of Christ that tends to bring out the crazy in people's theology. Somebody always wants to play "Pin the Tail on the Antichrist," or to hot-wire biblical prophecies to global politics, or to predict the exact date when the world will end.

Church history provides countless examples of end-time predictions. It happened in the Middle Ages, when one of the best-selling books was *Fifteen Signs of Doomsday*. It happened during the Reformation, when a German tailor declared himself "the Messiah of the Last Days" and announced that the whole world was about to be destroyed . . . except for his home city of Munster, where he would be king.[6]

It happens in America, too. Back in the nineteenth century the Millerites sold everything they owned, said their good-byes, and gathered on local hillsides to greet the coming of Christ, which they were certain would take place on October 22, 1844. At the end of the twentieth century everyone was reading *The Late Great Planet Earth*, which said the world would end in 1981.[7] That year came and went, but soon somebody else published *88 Reasons Why the Rapture Will Be in 1988*.[8] The book sold five million copies.

Given this history, it is not hard to understand why secular people get cynical about the second coming. But there is a danger for Christians as well, and that is to lose our sense of anticipation. Honestly, we are tempted to be apathetic. We know Jesus said that he is coming soon, but secretly we doubt that it will happen before we graduate from college, find a job, get married, start a family, or enjoy our retirement. Thus we are tempted to say what Peter warned that people would say in the last days: "Where is the promise of his coming?" (2 Pet. 3:4). Here is a simple test of your own expectations: did you wake up this morning with a hopeful anticipation that Jesus might return today, or has it been months and months since you prayed in faith for his kingdom to come?

What Not to Look For

A conversation in the Gospel of Luke helps us know how to live in hope for the kingdom of God. Like a lot of conversations in the Gospels, it started with a question: "Being asked by the Pharisees when the kingdom of God would come, he answered them, 'The kingdom of God is not coming in ways that can be observed, nor will they say, "Look, here it is!" or "There!"'" (Luke 17:20–21).

Jesus knew that the coming of the kingdom would tempt people to speculate about when it would arrive, and where it would come. So right from the beginning he warned people not to look for any signs or to make any predictions. Sure, the Bible gives many warning signs of the coming judgment: earthquakes, warfare, pestilence, and plague. These are all reminders that the kingdom is near. But they are not the kind of signs we can use to establish a timetable for the second coming.

After saying this to the Pharisees, Jesus repeated it to

his disciples: "The days are coming when you will desire to see one of the days of the Son of Man, and you will not see it. And they will say to you, 'Look, there!' or 'Look, here!' Do not go out or follow them" (Luke 17:22–23). When the Bible talks about the "day" or "days" of the Son of Man (e.g. Luke 17:22–30; Dan. 7:13–14), it is generally talking about the last day on earth, when Jesus will come again to judge the world.

Jesus was looking ahead to his future kingdom. He knew that as we waited and waited for that great day, wondering if it would ever come, some people would claim to have inside information. They would jump the gun and make predictions that were never part of God's plan. His message for us about this is very simple: we should not follow human prophecies that will only lead us to look for him in all the wrong places.

Besides, when Jesus does come again, it will happen so unexpectedly that it will be a total surprise. And it will happen so obviously that no one will be able to miss it. Jesus compared his coming to a sudden thunderbolt that streaks across the nighttime sky: "As the lightning flashes and lights up the sky from one side to the other, so will the Son of Man be in his day" (Luke 17:24). If that is true, then there is no need to speculate. Any sign would be superfluous. "At the end time of the world," said Cyril of Alexandria, "he will not descend from heaven obscurely or secretly, but with godlike glory."[9] Without a moment's notice, Christ will come to shake the world.

When Judgment Comes

If the prophecies of the second coming are true, then what should we do? After warning us not to speculate, Jesus gave some very practical advice about what to do in the meantime. If the kingdom is near, then we need to get ready, specifically by repenting of our sins.

To make this practical point, Jesus gave a couple of examples from the Old Testament—examples that show how unexpected the second coming will be, and also how terrible it will be for anyone who falls under the judgment of God.

The first example is the great flood: "Just as it was in the days of Noah, so will it be in the days of the Son of Man. They were eating and drinking and marrying and being given in marriage, until the day when Noah entered the ark, and the flood came and destroyed them all" (Luke 17:26–27; cf. Genesis 6–7).

It took Noah years to build his enormous ark. How preposterous it must have seemed for someone to build such a huge boat so far from any large body of water. No one paid him any attention, or if they did, it was only to make fun of him. People simply went about their business as usual: eating and drinking and marrying and doing all the other things that people do, but never turning away from their sins.

Then came the day when Noah went into his ark, with all God's animals. It started to rain, and it kept rain-ing until the floods came and everyone was washed away. The people who died never saw it coming. Jesus said the same thing will happen at the coming of his kingdom. People will be walking to class, or sitting down for dinner, or checking Facebook. They will be loving, or fighting, or serving, or sinning. And they will be taken totally by surprise.

Consider a second example, also from Genesis: "Likewise, just as it was in the days of Lot—they were eating and drinking, buying and selling, planting and building, but on the day when Lot went out from Sodom, fire and sulfur rained from heaven and destroyed them all" (Luke 17:28–29).

To this day, the sins of Sodom are infamous: injustice, inhospitality, immorality—especially flagrant sexual sin. Day after day the Sodomites kept on sinning, never imagining that God would destroy them. On the very day when fire fell from heaven, they were striking business deals and breaking ground on new construction. Suddenly they perished—every last one of them. Even Lot's wife was destroyed. With longing in her heart, she took one last look back at Sodom and she was turned into a pillar of salt (Gen. 19:26). The problem was not where she looked, but what she loved. The pleasures of sin were her fatal attraction.

According to Jesus, these stories are meant to be a warning for us! "Remember Lot's wife," he said. "So will it be on the day when the Son of Man is revealed" (Luke 17:30, 32). At the final lightning strike, judgment will come without warning. People will be practicing the piano, or studying for a biology test, or getting cash from the ATM when they are overtaken by the wrath of God.

How to Save Your Life

Will you be ready when the time comes? Most people aren't ready, because no matter how many warnings are given, they never listen. Sadly, at the end there will be nothing they can do to escape disaster. They will not even have time to check their text messages, because they never came to Christ while they still had the time. They never put their trust in the Savior who suffered rejection and crucifixion for sinners, whose kingdom only comes by way of the cross.

Jesus said, "Whoever seeks to preserve his life will lose it, but whoever loses his life will keep it" (Luke 17:33). This is one of the strange paradoxes of the gospel. If you try to save your life—in other words, if you hold on to this world and what it seems to offer—you will end up losing your life itself and everything you have worked so hard to gain.

On the other hand, if you give yourself away—if you commit your life to Christ and then pour yourself out in service to others—then you will get to keep your life forever. People may think you're crazy for doing it, but when you let go of what earth has to offer, you gain what only heaven has to give.

So what are you still trying to salvage from this fallen

world? What sins is your heart looking back to instead of leaving behind?

What you choose makes a difference. The kingdom is near, and when Jesus comes again he will make an eternal separation. Some will be saved, while others will be lost forever. Jesus put it as vividly as he could: "I tell you, in that night there will be two in one bed. One will be taken and the other left. There will be two women grinding grain together. One will be taken and the other left" (Luke 17:34–35).

Possibly Jesus meant that one person will be taken to glory, while the other will get left behind. Or maybe one person will be taken away to judgment, while the other is spared. Either way, God will divide the human race right down the center and make a final separation between the redeemed and the damned. This will separate even the closest relationships: students who share the same dorm room, colleagues who work in the same department, the neighbors who share the same fence. People in almost the exact same situation in life will find themselves on opposite sides of eternity.

It will happen any time now. If you are trusting in Christ, there is no need to be afraid. In fact, the reason Jesus gave us such clear warnings about the coming judgment is that he wants us to be saved. But if you are not holding on to his cross, then you are not ready for his return.

The famous evangelist Donald Grey Barnhouse used to tell the story of a man he went to visit in the hospital.

Dr. Barnhouse heard that one of his neighbors in Philadel-phia was dying, and since he knew that the man wasn't a Christian, he wanted one last chance to give him the gospel.

Sadly, even on his deathbed, the man showed little or no concern for his eternal destiny. Dr. Barnhouse decided that his desperate situation called for drastic measures. He asked the man if he could stay in his hospital room all night. When the man asked why, the evangelist pulled up a chair next to the bed, looked into the face of his friend, and said, "Because I've never seen a man die without Christ." Suddenly the man realized that he wasn't as ready to die as he thought he was. By the time their conversation was over, he repented of his sins and prayed to receive Jesus as his Savior and Lord. He was ready for kingdom come.

The kingdom is near for all of us—nearer than we think. The way to be ready is to do what Jesus said: repent and believe the gospel.

2

Mine Is the Kingdom

The kingdom is near. We know this because Jesus said it again and again: "The kingdom of God has come near to you" (Luke 10:9). "The time is fulfilled, and the kingdom of God is at hand; repent and believe in the gospel" (Mark 1:15).

When some people hear this, they want to know exactly how near the kingdom is. Their main interest is the kingdom's timing. For example, one cartoon depicts two men on a sidewalk holding signs announcing the coming of the kingdom. One sign reads, "The End Is Near," while the other says, "The End Is Thursday." The man with the more open-ended sign looks at his colleague, who has tied his prediction to one particular day, and thinks to himself, "Amateur!" And he's right: we do not know on which day the world will end. Jesus made it perfectly clear that *no one* knows when his kingdom will come. So why speculate?

Besides, when it comes to the kingdom, there is a

much more important question for us to consider than its timing. That question is whether we even *want* the kingdom to come. We say that we are for Christ and for his kingdom, yet often we are tempted to seek an alternative dominion.

The reason for this is very simple: we would rather rule our own lives than submit to the sovereignty of God. To accept Christ as King is to acknowledge his authority over every aspect of our lives. This is what a king is: someone who rules. So if Christ is king, then he has the right to rule over everything we are and have: our career plans, our wardrobe, our cell phone usage, our free time, our friend group. There is not one place in life where we can say, "This is for me, God, and not for you." So as we consider the kingship of Christ, the issue for us is not so much *when* his kingdom will come, but whether we want it to come at all.

I Will Be King!

One way to illustrate the choice we all have to make is to consider one of the Bible's most brutally honest verses. It comes from the story of Solomon, whom God had anointed be the king after David.

It so happened that in the days when David was so old that he had trouble keeping warm in bed, his oldest son Adonijah decided that he wanted to be the next king. Adonijah knew that God had chosen his younger brother Solomon instead. But rather than submitting to

God and his anointed one, he wanted his own kingdom. So he "exalted himself, saying, 'I will be king.'" But that is not all that Adonijah did. He also "prepared for himself chariots and horsemen, and fifty men to run before him" (1 Kings 1:5).

This incident is reminiscent of what happens in a game of checkers when one of the ordinary playing pieces suddenly becomes royalty. Having reached the far side of the board, a checker is crowned as king. "King me!" commands one of the players. A second checker is carefully stacked on top of the first checker, and from then on the newly crowned king has the power to move all over the board.

This is what Adonijah was doing when he exalted himself over Israel. "King me!" he said. Not even waiting for his father to die, he tried to take by force something that was only God's to give. Rather than submitting to the kingdom of God, Adonijah was seeking his own kingdom, by his own power, for his own glory. "Mine is the kingdom!" he was saying.

Have you ever felt the same temptation—to take what you want when you want it instead of waiting for what God wants to give you? In one way or another, we are all tempted to exalt ourselves. But when we put ourselves on the throne, God is no longer our King; he becomes one of our servants. Rather than seeking his kingdom, we expect him to seek ours.

Know this: if you decide to "king" yourself, sooner or

later you will get upset with God for not doing whatever it is that you expect him to do. When you are angry at the world, or angry with other people, or angry with God, it is almost always because the wrong person is on the throne.

It is instructive to notice how Adonijah exalted himself. The Scripture says that he started by gathering horses and chariots, with a charioteer to drive each one, and with fifty extra men to run ahead of him. If you want people to know how important you are, it helps to have your own entourage. That way, even before you arrive, people know that someone important is on the way.

Adonijah's entourage reminds me of a scene I witnessed in high school. It was freshman year, and our class had organized an auction to raise funds. Various freshmen sold themselves as slaves for a day. One enterprising sophomore spent chump change on some reasonably muscular football players and then paid top dollar for two of the prettiest girls in our class. When he came into French class the next day, he made a dramatic entrance. The guys were bearing him on a litter—like some teenage Pharaoh—while the girls fed him grapes one by one and fanned him with palm fronds.

Image is everything. If you are going to be the king, you have to act like the king, which includes having people treat you like the king. So Adonijah paid his posse. He also made sure he had the public support of some of Israel's most powerful leaders: the head of the military and one of the leading priests. Then he made a public display of personal wealth and religious commitment: "Adonijah sacrificed sheep, oxen, and fattened cattle . . . and he invited all his brothers, the king's sons, and all the royal officials of Judah" (1 Kings 1:9).

Basically, Adonijah was hosting his own coronation. He was getting the right people on his side, killing the fatted calf, throwing a huge party. At the same time, by making animal sacrifices he was giving the impression that he was deeply spiritual. Yet Adonijah was doing it all for himself. What makes this especially ironic is that his name means "God Is Master." However, what Adonijah really wanted was to be his own master, so he never submitted to the kingdom of God.

We are tempted to "king" ourselves the same way. We try to impress people with what we have, who we know, and how much we are doing for God. We like to have people around us who will tell us what we want to hear—reinforcing our attitudes, affirming our choices, and supporting our ambitions without ever challenging our perspective or correcting our sins.

Even if we never ride a chariot, hire fifty servants, or invite celebrities over for dinner, we find other ways to "king" ourselves. We make sure people know our test scores, tell everyone about our promotion at work, show off our latest purchases, brag about our kids, or do whatever people do in our community to keep score. Maybe we simply fuel our sense of self-importance by complaining about our workload. These are all ways of saying, "Mine is the kingdom." Like Adonijah, we try to give people the impression that we are something more than we really are.

The Kingdoms We Serve

As the servants of Christ, we are called to seek a different kingdom. Before considering some practical ways to do this, we should recognize some of the kingdoms we are tempted to seek instead. The better we understand these temptations, the more consistently we will be able to live for the kingdom of Jesus Christ.

To seek is to set your heart on something, to make it your main objective. What you seek is what you think about; it is what you pursue or live for. Many of us are tempted to seek *the kingdom of success*. What makes us feel good is being recognized for our achievements. We cannot really be happy unless we get the grade we think we deserve, give the performance we expect to give, or win the award we counted on winning. Maybe we thought we were doing it for the glory of God, but when we fail to live up to our standards, and suffer bitter disappointment as a result, we discover that what we really worshiped was success. Have you learned how to be second-best at something for the glory of God, if that's the best you can do, or is it killing you to know that someone else is better?

Most of us are also tempted to seek what Mark Buchanan calls *the kingdom of stuff*.[1] We live in a culture that believes there is always something we can buy that will make us happy. Just look at the way advertising sells happiness for the price of a new pair of sneakers. Better yet, think of all the stuff you end up dumping, storing, or leaving behind every time you move. Most Americans have more belongings in their bedrooms than the average Third World family has in their entire home—if they have one, which many people don't.

It is not wrong to own property, any more than it is wrong to succeed. But we need to remember how hard it is for rich people to enter the kingdom of heaven—harder, Jesus said, than "for a camel to go through the eye of a needle" (Matt. 19:24). And we need to recognize how tempting it is to worship things that we can buy. We give them our time. We pay them our money. We use them to establish our identity. Really, this is all simply another way of saying that we worship them. And when we do this, we are seeking the wrong kingdom.

In the end, of course, stuff never satisfies. To give one example, consider Mat Honan's lament over his disappointment with digital technology:

> There is a hole in my heart dug deep by advertising and envy and a desire to see a thing that is new and different and beautiful. A place within me that is empty, and that I want to fill up. The hole makes me think electronics can help. And of course, they can.
>
> They make the world easier and more enjoyable. They boost productivity and provide entertainment and information and sometimes even status. At least for

a while. At least until they are obsolete. At least until
they are garbage. . . . [I]n them we find entertainment
in lieu of happiness, and exchanges in lieu of actual
connections.

And oh, I am guilty. I am guilty. I am guilty.[2]

Then there is the *kingdom of sex*. This too is something
that we are tempted to worship. Whether they are gay or
straight, most people in our culture claim the right to use
their bodies any way they please. If it feels good, do it! Thus
they are offended by the very idea that anyone else has the
right to tell them how they should or shouldn't use their
sexual parts—even God Almighty. A good example comes
from television host Piers Morgan, who said that when it
comes to sex, we need to "move with the times" and drag
the Bible "kicking and screaming into the modern world."[3]
In other words, sex is sovereign, not God.

These are the kingdoms that people seek: sex, stuff,
success. Then add one more to the list. It may be the biggest kingdom of all: *the kingdom of self*. What keeps us from
saying to God, "Thine is the kingdom," is our stubborn
insistence on saying, "Mine is the kingdom!" Given the
choice, we want to enjoy our own pleasures, choose our
own entertainments, control our own schedules, and de-
termine our own destinies.

In a whimsical moment, I once took the classic hymn
"Have Thine Own Way, Lord!" and wrote a paraphrase. It
went like this:

34

Have mine own way, Lord! Have mine own way!
Let me be in charge here, at least for today.
I really don't need you—say what you will;
I've got my own plan, Lord; you can just chill!

Most of us would never put it that bluntly, of course, but that is often the way we operate: as if we are on the throne and God should be serving us. We do this because we are so in love with ourselves.

I am sometimes asked about my biggest regret from college. Was there something I never did but wished that I had done? What would I do differently if I could do it all over again? My biggest regret was that I loved myself too much to really love people the way that Jesus loves. This is what happens to all of us when we seek the kingdom of self.

Putting the Kingdom First

There is a different kingdom that God wants us to seek: the kingdom of the Lord Jesus Christ. Rather than crowning ourselves, Jesus invites us to submit to his sovereign rule and swear allegiance to his royal kingship. He calls us to surrender everything to him by putting his kingdom first. Remember what he said to his disciples: "Seek first the kingdom of God and his righteousness" (Matt. 6:33).

Remember as well that this commandment comes with a promise. Jesus said that if we seek his kingdom first, then "all these things will be added" to us (Matt. 6:33).

What he meant by "these things" were all the things that his disciples were worried about: food, clothing, and the necessities of daily life. If we pursue the kingdom of God, then God will give us everything we truly need.

But what does it mean to *seek* the kingdom? Consider the kingdoms we have just considered—the kingdoms that get in the way of the kingdom of God—and see how each area of life gets totally transformed when we surrender it to the kingship of Jesus Christ.

Start with *success*. What happens when we surrender the idol of success to the kingship of Christ? The main thing that ought to happen is this: we no longer base our sense of identity on what we achieve, or fail to achieve. Instead, we find our identity in the fact that we have a King who loves us and gave himself for us. This is something that no other religion can claim. Our loving Savior—the Lord Jesus Christ—lived for us, died for us, and rose again for us. This is the gospel, and it means we no longer live to gain anything for ourselves. For us, success means being faithful—faithful to use our gifts to the best of our ability for Christ and for his kingdom.

Then consider our *stuff*. If we are living for the right kingdom, then every choice we make about material possessions will be driven by our commitment to Christ. As citizens of God's kingdom, we have a simple criterion to use in making decisions about what to spend: Can I buy this for Christ and for his kingdom?

Rather than asking questions like, "Do I look good in

this?" or, "Would that be fun to do?" we will ask deeper questions like, "How will having this affect my relationships inside and outside the body of Christ?" or, "Given the work of the kingdom worldwide, is this the best way to use this money?"

Unless we ask these kinds of questions, it is hard for us to exercise good stewardship. At the same time, it is easy for us to be discontent. If we do not think carefully about our stewardship, we will always want more and never be satisfied with what we have. Understand that the way to be content is not by getting more of what we think we want, but by knowing when to say, "Enough is enough!"

One good way to test whether we are living for the kingdom of stuff is to consider how often we say "thank you" to God. When we sit down to a meal, do we take a few moments to thank God for the privilege of eating such nourishing and delicious food? Do we ever look around our homes and offer praise to God for our clothes, our books, our furniture, and whatever else we happen to own?

Mark Buchanan writes about the lessons he learned about gratitude through visiting a little township in Uganda. The local congregation worshiped on a dirt floor under a tin roof in a lean-to on the edge of a cornfield. One Sunday evening, the pastor asked if anyone had anything to share.

One woman stood up and said, "Oh, brothers and sisters, I love Jesus so much."

"Tell us, sister! Tell us!" demanded the congregation.

"Oh, I love him so much, I don't know where to begin to tell you how good he is."

"Begin there, sister!" they said. "Begin right there!"

"Oh, he is so good to me. I praise him all the time for how good he is to me. For three months, I prayed to the Lord for shoes. And look!" The woman lifted her leg so that everyone could see one foot, covered with an ordinary-looking shoe. "He gave me shoes. Hallelujah, he is so good."

Buchanan was devastated. "I sat there," he wrote, "hollowed out, hammered down. In all my life I had not once prayed for shoes. And in all my life I had not once thanked God for the many, many shoes I had."[4] Using our stuff for the kingdom of God starts with receiving it as a gift from God. This helps us remember that it is really for him and ought to be used for his glory.

Sex is designed to work the same way. Take it for ourselves, or take it from others, and it will still give us physical pleasure, but at the same time it will shrivel our soul. Sex is really about relationships. It is the covenant cement that God designed to unite one man and one woman in a love relationship for life. As the poet Wendell Berry once said, marriage is "the way we protect the possibility that sexual love can become a story."[5] That story is not just about us, it is really about Jesus, because the ultimate mystery of sex is to point us to Christ and our romance with him.

Seeking God's kingdom in our sexuality means saying, "Lord Jesus, I want this part of my life to be what you want it to be, not what I want it to be. Sex is not outside my commitment to your kingdom, but inside. So I surrender my sexual thoughts, sexual desires, and the sexual parts of my body to your sovereignty. Use them to bring me closer to you, not take me farther away."

The Final Surrender

But why stop with our sexuality? If we are putting the kingdom first in everything else—if we are seeking the kingdom of God rather than the kingdoms of sex, or stuff, or success—then why not offer him our very selves? Seeking the kingdom of Christ means surrendering the kingdom of *self*.

For most of us, this is the hardest kingdom to leave behind. The reason we strive for success, and accumulate so much stuff, and violate God's holy standard for sexual purity is because Self is on the throne. We are like Adonijah, who said, "I will be king!" Instead of living like Joseph of Arimathea, who was "looking for the kingdom of God" (Luke 23:51), we are more like Diotrephes, whom the New Testament describes as someone "who likes to put himself first" (3 John 9).

For some of us, selfishness comes in negative forms. We are prone to self-pity, or even self-loathing. The problem is not just what we are thinking about ourselves, but also our constant self-focus. We are too self-absorbed.

Some of us think more positively about ourselves, but this too is a problem because we are guilty of self-promotion and self-gratification—anything that starts with "self."

We need to see ourselves the way God sees us: as beloved sons and daughters who cannot possibly be loved any more than we already are. Then we will stop thinking so much about ourselves and think more about others, and more about the kingdom of God. Then we will learn to say what the first Christians said when they "turned the world upside down" by resisting the temptations of a pagan culture: "There is another King, Jesus" (Acts 17:6–7).

The king we serve renounced every selfish claim so that he could serve us. His sacrificial death is our salvation. And now serving his kingdom is our joy.

One man who understood what it means to seek the kingdom first was the famous evangelist John Wesley. If we are wise, we will surrender our lives to Christ the way that Wesley did, when he prayed:

> I am no longer my own, but yours. Put me to what you will, rank me with whom you will; put me to doing, put me to suffering; let me be employed for you or laid aside for you, exalted for you or brought low for you; let me be full, let me be empty; let me have all things, let me have nothing; I freely and wholeheartedly yield all things to your pleasure and disposal.[6]

3

Thy Kingdom Come

No matter how near we are to the kingdom of God, there are times when we are too busy building our own kingdom to seek his kingdom. We live for the kingdom of success, the kingdom of stuff, or the kingdom of sex rather than the kingdom of Jesus Christ.

But there are also times when our hearts ache with longing for the coming of the kingdom of God. Instead of saying, "Mine is the kingdom!" we turn back to God and say, "*Yours* is the kingdom and the power and the glory." We catch some passing glimpse of the eternal beauty of Jesus Christ, and this gives us a pure desire for his kingdom to come.

Our desperate longing for a better world can be well illustrated from a famous scene in the movie *The Shawshank Redemption*. Ellis Boyd Redding has been sentenced to life in prison at Shawshank State Penitentiary. One day his friend Andy defies the threat of solitary confinement by locking himself into the communication center and playing opera music over the prison loudspeaker: a duet from Mozart's *Le Nozze di Figaro*.

For Redding and his fellow prisoners, listening to such beautiful music is a liberating experience. In the cinematic voiceover, he says:

> I have no idea to this day what those two Italian ladies were singin' about. . . . I like to think they were singin' about something so beautiful it can't be expressed in words, and makes your heart ache because of it. I tell you those voices soared, higher and farther than anybody in a gray place dares to dream. It was like some beautiful bird flapped into our drab little cage and made these walls dissolve away, and for the briefest of moments, every last man at Shawshank felt free.[1]

Like Ellis Redding, we have heard the soaring music. We have seen and heard things so beautiful that they make our hearts ache with longing for God: the yellow leaf on the mossy bank, an eagle dancing on the wind, the first sweet notes of a haunting melody, the warm embrace that follows a sin forgiven and a relationship reconciled. These adumbrations of eternity awaken our desire to be with Christ and to see the coming of his kingdom. So we say, "Come, Lord Jesus!"

Praying for the Kingdom

Notice that these words from Scripture come in the form of a prayer. This is so important that Jesus made it one of the main petitions in the daily prayer he taught to his disciples: "Your kingdom come, your will be done, on earth as it is in heaven" (Matt. 6:10). The coming of the kingdom is something to pray for.

Prioritizing prayer stands in contrast to many other things that people try to do with the kingdom of God. Christians often talk about advancing or extending the kingdom of God. Sometimes we do this by pursuing a political agenda. Other times we do it through evangelism or missionary work. But however we do it, we are tempted to think of the kingdom of Jesus Christ as something that we accomplish. If we build it, he will come.

This is not quite the biblical way of looking at things. The Bible generally does not talk about us "creating" or "advancing" the kingdom of God. This is because establishing the kingdom is primarily something God does, not something we do. James Davison Hunter cautions that when Christians

> participate in the work of world-building they are not, in any precise sense of the phrase, "building the Kingdom of God." This side of heaven, the culture cannot become the Kingdom of God, nor will all the work of Christians in culture evolve into or bring about his Kingdom. The establishment of his Kingdom in eternity is an act of divine sovereignty and love and it will only be set in place at the final consummation at the end of time.[2]

When it comes to understanding God's role and our role in bringing the kingdom, the Lord's Prayer should be our first clue. The reason we *pray* for the kingdom is because we are totally dependent on God to establish it. The way for Christ to have a kingdom is not for us to build it, but for him to bring it.

We know this from the Lord's Prayer, and also from the verbs the Bible uses to talk about the kingdom in other places. When Paul described how we enter the kingdom, he did not talk about what we do, but about what God does: "He has delivered us from the domain of darkness and transferred us to the kingdom of his beloved Son" (Col. 1:13). The apostle spoke the same way about his own entrance to the kingdom—not just the kingdom of grace he entered when he put his faith in Christ, but the kingdom of glory he would gain when he died. Here was Paul's testimony: "The Lord will rescue me from every evil deed and bring me safely into his heavenly kingdom. To him be the glory forever" (2 Tim. 4:18).

Peter talked about the kingdom in the same way. He did not describe it as a human enterprise, but as a divine gift: "There will be richly provided for you an entrance into the eternal kingdom of our Lord and Savior Jesus Christ" (2 Pet. 1:11).

The reason the apostles talked about the kingdom like this is because that is the way Jesus talked about it. Jesus did not tell his disciples to build, establish, or advance the kingdom. Instead, he told them to *receive* it. "Fear not, little flock," he said, "for it is your Father's good pleasure to give you the kingdom" (Luke 12:32).

All of this helps explain why we pray for the kingdom to come. It is a gift of God's grace, which we receive by faith. The kingdom comes through the life, death, and resurrection of Jesus Christ. Thus it is not something God wants us to work with our hands to achieve; it is something he wants us to open our hands to receive.

Consider how extraordinary it is that God would give us a kingdom. We would be amazed if someone were to give us something as big as a house. But here God comes, giving away entire kingdoms. And he is happy to do it. Never think for a moment that God is too stingy to give you what you truly need. According to Jesus, it is our Father's good pleasure to give us his entire kingdom.

Repenting and Believing

How should we pray for the kingdom to come? We start with our personal prayers of repentance and faith. Before we pray for the kingdom to come to anyone else, we pray that it would come to us.

Jesus made this clear the first time he preached the kingdom of God. As he began his public ministry, he started by saying, "The kingdom of God is at hand," and then the very next thing he said was, "Repent and believe in the gospel" (Mark 1:15). Jesus put the same things together in the Lord's Prayer: "Your kingdom come" goes with "Forgive us our debts."

Have you asked Jesus to bring you into the kingdom of God? We do this by repenting of our allegiance to all kinds of other kingdoms. "Lord Jesus," we say, "I renounce my love for the kingdoms of this world. I confess that for too long I have lived for my own selfish pleasures. I turn my back on the idol of success, the lust of my flesh, and all the meaningless stuff that I desire to possess. And I come asking your forgiveness through the blood that you shed for me on the cross."

We cannot gain entrance to the kingdom by claiming our righteousness; we can only receive it by confessing our sinfulness. If we never do this, we will never enter the kingdom. Jesus was as clear about this as he was about anything. "Unless you repent," he said, "you will all . . . perish" (Luke 13:3, 5). So our prayer for the kingdom to come begins with confessing our sins.

Consider this good old Puritan prayer of repentance:

Holy Lord,
I have sinned times without number,
    and been guilty of pride and unbelief,
    of failure to find thy mind in thy Word,
    of neglect to seek thee in my daily life.
My transgressions and short-comings
    present me with a list of accusations,
But I bless thee that they will not stand against me,
    for all have been laid on Christ.[3]

This is the way that we should pray: fully acknowledging our sin, but at the same time totally trusting in Jesus. When our Savior said that the kingdom was at hand, he didn't just say, "Repent." He also said, "Believe the gospel." So we come into his kingdom by faith as well as repentance.

There are many ways to offer this kind of prayer. We can pray what some people call "The Sinner's Prayer," which is really any prayer in which we confess our sin and place our personal trust in Jesus Christ. A good example comes from *The Pilgrim's Progress*, by John Bunyan, in which Hopeful tells Christian to pray like this:

> God be merciful to me a sinner, and make me to know and believe in Jesus Christ. . . . Lord, I have heard that thou art a merciful God, and hast ordained that thy Son Jesus Christ should be the Savior of the world; and moreover, that thou art willing to bestow him upon such a poor sinner as I am—and I am a sinner indeed. Lord, take therefore this opportunity, and magnify thy grace in the salvation of my soul, through thy Son Jesus Christ. Amen.[4]

If this good prayer sounds a little too complicated, we can simply pray the way the thief prayed on the cross the day that Christ was crucified. As he was dying, right next to Jesus, the man came under the conviction of his sin. He testified that his condemnation was just, that he was being executed for crimes he had actually committed. But before he died, he put his trust in Christ. He turned to the Savior and prayed, "Jesus, remember me when you come into your kingdom" (Luke 23:42). The kingdom was near to that man—so near that Jesus said to him, "Today you will be with me in Paradise" (v. 43). In this way, the thief on the cross repented, believed, and was saved.

Whatever words we use, we need to put our trust in Jesus. Otherwise, we will never enter the kingdom. I first learned this lesson when I was a little boy and my father would read me Bible stories at bedtime. One of the earliest stories I remember is Nicodemus coming to Jesus by night. Maybe I remember this story because it was bedtime, when the lights were dim and starlight was coming in through the windowpane.

It was easy to imagine Jesus and Nicodemus talking together on a warm summer's night, maybe on a rooftop. And I heard what Jesus said to his friend: "Truly, truly, I say to you, unless one is born again he cannot see the kingdom of God" (John 3:3). Then he said it again, "Unless one is born of . . . the Spirit, he cannot enter the kingdom of God" (v. 5).

As I heard the story, I wanted to come to Jesus, too, and meet him the way that Nicodemus did. Jesus seemed like the best friend a boy could ever have. And though I hardly knew what it meant, I wanted to be born again. By the power of the Spirit, the words of Jesus resonated in the chambers of my heart: "I must be born again!"

The same thing is true for everyone. The kingdom has to be in us before we can be in the kingdom.[5] So, if we want to see the kingdom come, we must ask the Holy

Spirit to make us born again. This is the way the kingdom comes: through repentance and faith.

Kingdom Prayer

We do not stop there, however. When the kingdom comes to us, we want it to come to others, too. "Thy kingdom come" is not a selfish prayer. It is a prayer for God to bring the nations under his gracious rule—to send the Holy Spirit with the power of new birth and the gifts of repentance and faith.

Remember, our first calling is not to build the kingdom, but to pray for the kingdom to come. So what place does this kind of intercession have in your prayer life? Most of us spend a fair amount of time offering what might be called "emergency prayer." The things that really motivate us to pray are the things that we feel desperate about. As a result, God hears a lot about our physical problems, our financial needs, and whatever struggles we are having in our daily work.

These are all good things to pray about. There is nothing wrong with emergency prayer. Our Father loves to hear what we need, and then provide it. But prayer can be so much more. At least some of our petitions should be for God's kingdom to come. Part of our calling as Christians is to pray for Christ to be the King.

Call this kind of prayer "kingdom prayer." Kingdom prayer is explicitly directed toward the greater glory of God. It is prayer for the unhindered expansion and unlimited extension of his rule. It is prayer for missions and evangelism, for pastors and churches, for towns and cities, for nations and people groups. It is prayer for people who are lost to find their salvation in Jesus Christ.

Add kingdom prayer to all the emergency items on your prayer list. Pray consistently for one person to be born again. Pray faithfully for the preaching ministry of your local church. Pray knowledgeably for the work of a missionary or evangelist.

God loves to answer kingdom prayer. Hudson Taylor, the pioneer missionary to China, was mystified by the large number of souls being won to Christ at one of his mission stations. The mystery was solved on a trip back home to England. A man came up after a public address and began asking what God was doing at that mission station. The man was so conversant with the work there that Taylor asked him how he knew so much about it. "Oh!" he replied, "the missionary there and I are old college mates; for years he has sent me the names of inquirers and converts, and these I have daily taken to God in prayer."[6]

One of the reasons we sometimes doubt the power of God is because we do not see him doing anything in the world. But sometimes we do not see what he is doing because we don't notice it, and we don't notice it because we haven't been looking to see the answers to our prayers—not just for the little things of daily life, but the more important priorities of the kingdom. F. B. Meyer said, "Whenever we so lose ourselves in prayer as to forget personal interest, and to plead for the glory of God, we have reached a vantage ground from which we can win anything from Him."[7]

Anxious for Nothing

When you commit your life to kingdom prayer, something remarkable happens—something that makes a practical difference in everyday life. People who seek the kingdom of God—and who therefore pray in faith for its coming—are set free from anxiety to live with generosity.

Most of us experience a lot more anxiety in life than we need to, and this makes us much less generous than we ought to be. We get stressed out by all the work that we still need to do; we are not sure how or even if we can get it all done. We worry what people will think of us, so we get nervous in certain social situations. There are things we need but don't have. We have a lot of unanswered questions about the future. People we care about have problems we have no idea how to fix. Life in a fallen world is anxiety producing. Indeed, sometimes it can be overwhelming.

Yet Jesus tells us not to worry about anything. "Why are you anxious?" he wants to know. "Do not be anxious," he tells us, "nor be worried" (Luke 12:22, 29).

To prove his point, Jesus uses examples from the natural world—creatures that he made and keeps under his care. "Consider the ravens," he says (vv. 24–26), and, "Consider the lilies" (vv. 27–28). The ravens get everything they need to eat, even though they know nothing about farming. Similarly—and here Jesus turns from ornithology to botany—the field lilies are adorned with beauty, even though they have never learned how to sew.

This is an argument from the lesser to the greater. Ravens are clever, but not very attractive. They are like crows, only bigger—great squawking creatures with fierce eyes and at times an ill temper. Lilies are very fragile. When the weather is dry and the wind blows, they soon disappear. Nevertheless, God provides for the lilies and the ravens alike. If he takes care of birds and wildflowers, he will certainly take care of you. This is the point. Because he is your Father, and because you are the child that he loves, he will give you good things to eat and good clothes to wear, just like the lilies and the ravens.

How unnecessary it is—indeed, how absurd it is—for us to be anxious about things that God has promised to provide. Worry gains us nothing, and therefore we are anxious for nothing, as Jesus went on to say: "And which of you by being anxious can add a single hour to his span of life? If then you are not able to do as small a thing as that, why are you anxious about the rest?" (Luke 12:25–26). If only we had one more hour in the day, one more day in the week, one more week in the year! But we will not get anything more by worrying about it. All our worrying will not help us one little bit.

In fact, far from adding anything, anxiety always subtracts. Worry is a thief. It steals our time. Our thoughts turn to our troubles, and then rather than praying about them or doing the things God is calling us to do, we waste time worrying about them. Worry steals our rest. We lie awake at night, anxious about tomorrow, and then we get up too tired to work hard, and this only adds to our anxiety. Worry steals our obedience, as it tempts us to other sins like irritability, addiction, and laziness, or, on the other hand, overwork. Worry steals our hope, as we fear the worst about the future. All kinds of difficulties arise in our minds—most of which will never come to pass. What a sad waste it all is! Worry shrivels the soul, robbing our joy, leaving us ill-equipped to face the spiritual and emotional challenges of each new day. Few things are as discouraging to our spirit, or as destructive to our contentment, or as detrimental to our witness as the anxious worries of a troubled heart.

Seeking the Kingdom

Rather than worrying about everything all the time, therefore, Jesus wants us to do something else instead. He wants us to seek his kingdom. He wants "thy kingdom come" to become our lifestyle. Most people try to get whatever they can out of life. But our Father knows what we need. So Jesus tells us not to be afraid, but to seek his kingdom, sell our possessions, and give to the needy (Luke 12:31–33). When the kingdom comes first for us, we are liberated from the grasping pursuit of temporary things. We do not have to worry about what we need anymore, so we can give to others instead.

A good example of trusting God's provision comes from the founding of L'Abri, the evangelical retreat that Francis and Edith Schaeffer started in Switzerland. The Schaeffers believed that God had called them to make a home for young people who needed to find Christ. Yet their visas were about to expire, and unless they found a permanent residence, they would have to return to the United States without seeing their vision become a reality. It came down to the last day, and Edith prayed out loud for God to provide: "Oh, Heavenly Father . . . if You want us to stay in Switzerland, if Your word to me concerning L'Abri means our being in these mountains, then I know You are able to find a house, and lead me to it in the *next half hour*. Nothing is impossible to You. But You will have to do it."[8]

While she was praying, Mrs. Schaeffer heard someone in the street calling her name. It was a local real estate dealer wanting to know if she had found anything yet. Soon he was driving her to a mountain chalet that was unexpectedly unavailable. They had found the right house. But they still didn't have any money to pay for it. As Edith prayed in faith that night, she asked for a sign: "Oh, please show us Thy will about this house tomorrow, and if we are to *buy* it . . . send us one thousand dollars before ten o'clock tomorrow morning."[9]

The next morning a letter came with the post by train. It was from a couple that had been praying for the Schaeffers for many years, but had never supported them financially because they had so little to give. Yet they had unexpectedly come into some money. At first they thought about buying a new car, or a new house. But in the end they agreed to invest in the kingdom of God. So they sent the Schaeffers a check in the amount of—you guessed it— one thousand dollars!

This is what happens when people put the kingdom first. Instead of worrying, they pray. Instead of keeping, they give. This is not their loss, but their gain. It is because Jesus wants the best for us that he tells us to make "thy kingdom come" our daily prayer, and also our way of life.

4

The Forever Kingdom

The twenty-first century began with the United States of America firmly in place as the most dominant nation on earth. With the fall of the Berlin Wall and the end of the Cold War, the old Soviet Union had collapsed and Russia was in decline. China loomed on the horizon, but it was far behind the US in everything except population. Other nations were coming to terms with a one-superpower world.

Yet within a few short years, many Americans began to entertain serious doubts about the future. The first time I heard the name Osama bin Laden was at an outdoor dinner party with friends in Philadelphia sometime in the late 1990s. When I think of that happy evening today, a cold chill passes over me. Little did we suspect how profoundly that one man's animus would change American life.

Nor is 9/11 the only reversal that the United States has suffered. The wars in Iraq and Afghanistan lingered long past their "use by" date. The economic meltdown of 2008 revealed deep structural cracks in our financial system—cracks that widened under the weight of other international pressures. Political solutions have failed, and there is a consensus that Washington isn't working very well. Our society seems less secure. No one feels this more keenly than America's young people, whether they are still in school, looking for work, or occupying Wall Street.

If we didn't know it before—or if sometimes we were tempted to forget—America is not destined to last forever. This is hardly a surprise. Sooner or later, the mighty kingdoms of this world all fall down. Dictators like Hitler are overthrown. Military empires collapse, like ancient Assyria or imperial Rome. Dynasties come to an end, as we learn from the long succession of ruling families in Egypt and China. Eventually, even the benevolent monarchies and representative democracies fail.

How long will it be until the kingdom of America passes into history and people visit what is left of the Washington Monument the way they visit the Coliseum in Rome? Although only a prophet could tell us the number of days or weeks or years that America as we know it will survive, any thoughtful observer can readily see that national disaster is all but inevitable.

The eventual end of America is only one example of the wider principle that in this world all good things come to an end—everything from a college semester to a close friendship separated by death.

Even the world itself will come to an end. In his book

The God of Hope and the End of the World, the Cambridge physicist John Polkinghorne lists some of the dangers that threaten to extinguish life on earth: meteorites, black holes, nearby supernovas, deadly viruses and bacteria, nuclear war, environmental pollution, and the big freeze or the big crunch (depending on whether you think gravity or expansion will win out in the end). Polkinghorne concludes by saying that however the world will end, we have to take seriously the fact that catastrophe is coming, and include this reality in our view of the world.[1]

The Kingdom's Promise

As a worldview, Christianity takes all of this into account. We believe that one day the world will come to an end; every earthly kingdom will fail. But we also believe there is one kingdom that is built to last. The one good thing we know for certain will never come to an end is the forever kingdom of Jesus Christ. The kingdom to come—the kingdom we pray for and are called to seek—will endure forever.

This promise runs right through the story line of Scripture. God has always promised a kingdom. It started with King David, when God promised that his kingdom would never end. Here is the covenant that God made with David: "When your days are fulfilled and you lie down with your fathers, I will raise up your offspring after you, who shall come from your body, and I will establish his kingdom. He shall build a house for my name, and I will establish the throne of his kingdom forever" (2 Sam. 7:12–13). In case there was any doubt, God repeated this promise twice more in the same conversation: "Your house and your kingdom shall be made sure forever before me. Your throne shall be established forever" (v. 16).

So God established the house and the line of David as the one world dynasty that would never come to an end. In response, the Old Testament people of God believed that belonging to David's kingdom was a high privilege. God's royal promise was part of Israel's joyful praise. "They shall speak of the glory of your kingdom," the people sang, "and all your saints shall bless you." Why would the Israelites do this? Because, they said, "your kingdom is an everlasting kingdom, and your dominion endures throughout all generations" (Ps. 145:10, 11, 13).

There were times when God's people were tempted to doubt this promise. Israel was not always great among the nations. Sometimes God's people wondered if he had forgotten them. But there were always prophets who kept the promise alive. Think of Isaiah, for example. At a time of spiritual and political darkness, when hope grew dim, he prophesied a ruler who would come out of Galilee—a light for the nations. "For to us a child is born," he said, "to us a son is given; and the government shall be upon his shoulder, and his name shall be called Wonderful Counselor, Mighty God, Everlasting Father, Prince of Peace" (Isa. 9:6).

The language of Isaiah's prophecy made it clear that the coming Savior would be a ruler—someone to shoulder the burden of government. But Isaiah went on to make the amazing promise that this particular kingdom would last forever: "Of the increase of his government and of peace there will be no end, on the throne of David and over his kingdom, to establish it and to uphold it with justice and with righteousness from this time forth and forevermore" (Isa. 9:7).

The ancient prophets understood that the kingdom of the coming Christ would go from strength to strength. His governing power would never diminish, but grow and grow for all eternity.

This prophecy—the promise of a forever kingdom—runs right on through to the end of the Bible. The book of Revelation opens a window to heaven and shows us the worship of the angels and the saints in glory. In their ceaseless praise, they never grow weary of saying what have become the familiar words of the *Hallelujah Chorus*: "The kingdom of the world has become the kingdom of our Lord and of his Christ, and he shall reign forever and ever" (Rev. 11:15).

When we look at Scripture with a wide-angle lens, the kingdom promise fills our field of vision. God has always promised a kingdom that would last forever.

Mary's Prophecy

The forever kingdom came into sharper focus at the birth of Christ, with the remarkable promises that the angel Gabriel made to the Virgin Mary. Henry O. Tanner captures this moment in his famous painting *The Annunciation*.

Tanner was perhaps the first African-American artist to gain international acclaim. His travels to Palestine gave a robust realism to his paintings on biblical themes, and *The Annunciation* is no exception. Tanner's Mary is an ordinary girl in ordinary surroundings, wearing homespun clothes, sitting quietly in a room with dirty smudges on the wall.

But as plain as Mary is, there is a look of thoughtful wonderment on the young girl's face. The glory of an angel has invaded her personal space to reveal this extraordinary promise: "Behold, you will conceive in your womb and bear a son, and you shall call his name Jesus. He will be great and will be called the Son of the Most High. And the Lord God will give to him the throne of his father David, and he will reign over the house of Jacob forever, and of his kingdom there will be no end" (Luke 1:31–33).

Imagine the scene. Mary was just an ordinary girl, from an ordinary place. Though we do not know exactly how old she was, very likely she was a young teenager— think "high school freshman." She was living in the northern reaches of Israel, far from the center of national life in Jerusalem. Within the broader scope of international affairs, her hometown was a forgotten village on the outskirts of the mighty Roman Empire. How could anything important ever happen in Nazareth?

Yet here, suddenly, was the mightiest of angels. Gabriel's words were all but incomprehensible. To Mary (of all people) was promised the motherhood of the most important person who ever lived—the unique divine Son of God.

The angel said that Mary's son would be great. He said that the child would have a unique relationship to God. He would be called "the Son of the Most High," a title that David himself often used to testify to the greatness of God. Amazingly, though Mary lived far from anything resembling a court or a palace, her son would be royalty. By the will and purpose of Almighty God, he would sit on the throne of David, as his rightful heir. More amazing still, he would rule a forever kingdom. This promise was repeated to Mary for emphasis: "He will reign over the house of Jacob forever, and of his kingdom there will be no end" (Luke 1:33).

This infinity of a promise is essential to the message of Christmas, and therefore to the message of Christianity. At Christmastime we typically (and rightly) contemplate the mystery of the incarnation—that God became man. We praise his infinite condescension in exchanging the courts of heaven for a Bethlehem barn—deity in a manger. We marvel at his humility in suffering the frustration of life in a fallen world. People say there are two things in life that no one can avoid: death and taxes. Jesus could not avoid them, either. Humanly speaking, the reason he was born in Bethlehem was because Caesar believed there could be no taxation without registration. And everyone knows where Jesus died: on the cross of Calvary.

Thus the incarnation faces up to the hard realities of life: poverty, suffering, pain, and death. But it also opens up windows to eternity. Alongside all of the other things we know about the birth of Jesus Christ, we should never forget this: that he came to us with the promise of a forever kingdom. Put this label on the cradle in the stable: "King of Kings Forever and Ever."

Mary's Song

The kingdom of Jesus Christ is no temporary monarchy, and this changes everything. Mary understood this. She believed that God's kingdom is forever. We know this from the song that she sang to celebrate the Savior's birth. We call it "the Magnificat"—the psalm she composed in the weeks and months following the angel's announcement that she would give birth to a son.

As Mary sang from the heart, she praised God for doing things that only a king could do:

> My soul magnifies the Lord,
>   and my spirit rejoices in God my Savior,
> for he has looked on the humble estate of his servant.
>   For behold, from now on all generations will call
>   me blessed;
> for he who is mighty has done great things for me,
>   and holy is his name.
> And his mercy is for those who fear him
>   from generation to generation.
> He has shown strength with his arm;
>   he has scattered the proud in the thoughts of
>   their hearts;
> he has brought down the mighty from their thrones

and exalted those of humble estate;
he has filled the hungry with good things,
and the rich he has sent away empty.
He has helped his servant Israel,
in remembrance of his mercy,
as he spoke to our fathers,
to Abraham and to his offspring forever.
(Luke 1:46–55)

People sometimes wonder how a girl like Mary could write a song like this. In fact, some critics doubt that someone so unsophisticated could have produced such a spiritual and theological masterpiece.

We could answer, of course, by appealing to the power of the Holy Spirit. Like everything else in Scripture, Mary's song was written under divine inspiration. But we should also recognize God's work in her life. Mary was raised on the songs and hymns of the people of God. Like many other children in Israel, she knew the biblical psalms.

This explains why Mary's song sounds so familiar, like something we have heard before. Think of her psalm as a patchwork quilt. From the time she was a little girl, Mary had stored scraps of music in her heart—the poetry of the psalms. And not just the psalms: Mary alludes to or quotes from Genesis, Deuteronomy, Samuel, Job, Isaiah, Ezekiel, Micah, Habakkuk, and Zephaniah.[2] When the time came for her to receive God's kingdom promise, she stitched those scraps together into a fabric of praise.

Notice the way that Mary's song improvises on Gabriel's theme. The angel had promised that her son would become the king. In her song, Mary celebrates his mighty acts: scattering the proud, bringing down the mighty, feeding the hungry, helping his people. These deeds are worthy of a gracious King. Timothy Dudley-Smith captures the spirit of Mary's praise in a memorable paraphrase:

> Tell out my soul, the greatness of his might!
> Powers and dominions lay their glory by.
> Proud hearts and stubborn wills are put to flight,
> The hungry fed, the humble lifted high.[3]

But that is not all. Mary was also sure to mention that this kingdom is forever. *All* generations will look back to the birth of her son (Luke 1:48). From generation to generation, his mercy will be a blessing to everyone who trusts in him (v. 50). This promise goes all the way back to Abraham, but it also stretches forward to God's children forever (v. 55). In worshiping the King, Mary celebrated the eternality of his kingdom.

The Kingdom's Future

Mary's song contains some of the boldest lyrics in the Bible. She was a woman of faith, and as we hear her words, we sense her absolute confidence that God will do what he promised and send a Savior. This Savior will put everything right with the world. And when he does make everything right, it will stay right forever.

The promise of the forever kingdom puts all our problems into perspective and gives us hope in present trials. Think what this promise means for us as we seek the kingdom of God and pray for its coming.

It means that every wrong will be righted, every injustice rectified. As the Son of the Most High God, Mary's child has the power to put things back where they belong. If you long for justice, put your confidence in him. By the time that all is said and done, Jesus Christ will bring down every oppressor and set his captive people free. The hungry will be fed, and the rich—the ones who never lifted a finger to help anyone in need—will be banished from the kingdom of God. Here is how the London preacher Martyn Lloyd-Jones described the coming reversal:

> When the King of Kings and the Lord of Lords came into this world, he came into a stable. If you do not feel a sense of holy laughter within you, I do not see that you have a right to think that you are a Christian. Thank God, this is gospel, this is salvation. God turning upside down, reversing everything we have ever thought, everything we have taken pride in. The mighty? Why, he will pull them down from their seats. He has been doing so. He is still doing so. Let any man arise and say he is going to govern, to be the god of the whole world; you need not be afraid—he will be put down. Every dictator has gone down; they all do. Finally, the devil and all that belong to him will go down to the lake of fire and will be destroyed forever. The Son of God has come into the world to do that.[4]

The promise of the forever kingdom means as well that all of our troubles are only temporary. Usually when we are struggling with the pressures of life, they loom so large that we have trouble seeing beyond them. They are like the semi-truck that fills our rearview mirror. It is hard to believe the warning that says, "Objects may be closer than they appear," because all we can see is headlights and grillwork. Often our problems look the same way to us: so large that we can't see anything else, including God. But the promise of a forever kingdom expands our field of vision. It helps us see that eventually all our troubles will be over, and whatever struggles we have right now will give way to a trouble-free eternity. This does not make our problems less painful, of course, but it does put them into their proper perspective.

The forever kingdom also holds out the promise that we will live forever with the people we love. Sooner or later, we all lose people we care about. Our grief lingers long after their bodies have been buried in the ground. But we live in hope that we will see every believer again. A temporary kingdom makes no such promise. Once relationships are lost, they are lost forever. But the kingdom of God endures. And in that kingdom, the resurrection people of God are joined together again in glory, never to be separated again. Even if we are apart for now, our friendships in Christ will last forever.

Maybe best of all, the promise of a forever kingdom means that God will get the glory that he deserves. At the beginning, when Christ was born in Bethlehem, just a handful of shepherds worshiped him, plus several wise kings and a few godly old-timers who knew what to look for (not to mention a host of angels). But that was only the beginning. The worship of Jesus Christ that began with his incarnation will never end, because his kingdom will never end. Praise God, because this is nothing less than Jesus deserves: endless praise for his infinite kingship. "Therefore," says the writer to the Hebrews, "let us be grateful for receiving a kingdom that cannot be shaken, and thus let us offer to God acceptable worship, with reverence and awe" (Heb. 12:28).

Everyone who worships the Christ of the forever kingdom may pray in hope the way John Donne prayed. As that great English preacher and poet looked ahead to the infinite worship of God, he lifted up this beautiful prayer:

> Bring us, O Lord, at our last awakening into the house and gate of heaven, to enter into that gate and dwell in that house, where there shall be no darkness nor dazzling, but one equal light; no noise nor silence, but one equal music; no fears nor hopes, but one equal possession; no ends nor beginnings, but one equal eternity; in the habitation of thy glory and dominion, world without end.[5]

5

Missing the Kingdom

We belong to an eternal kingdom—a kingdom that is coming very soon. So we make the kingdom part of our daily prayers, saying, "Come, Lord Jesus, and with your kingdom, come!" And we live for the second coming of Jesus Christ, setting our hopes on the grace that will be brought to us at the end of the world.

At least, this is what we ought to do. Yet, if we are honest, we have to confess that we do not always want his kingdom to come. Sometimes it is easier for us to say "mine is the kingdom" than it is to live under the lordship of Jesus Christ. We are tempted to worship the kingdoms of this world instead—everything from the kingdom of stuff to the kingdom of self.

What makes this incredibly foolish is that none of these other kingdoms is built to last. Only one kingdom is eternal: the kingdom of our God, and of his Christ, who shall reign forever and ever. This kingdom reality changes everything. It means that all our problems are only temporary, and that everything we do for Jesus counts for eternity.

Know this: God has guaranteed everlasting joy for everyone who belongs to his kingdom. If this is true, then it is desperately important for us to hear what Jesus says in Luke 13—something much too important to leave out of our thinking about the coming of the kingdom of God. In this passage Jesus warns that some people will miss his kingdom entirely. Sadly, they will end up on the wrong side of eternity.

People who give directions often say, "You can't miss it!" (which usually turns out to be the kiss of death for actually finding the place). But when it came to the kingdom of God, Jesus said exactly the opposite. He said that it would be very easy to miss the kingdom. Jesus told us this out of grace and mercy because he does not want us to miss the kingdom; he wants us to enter in.

A Question of Salvation

Jesus talked about missing the kingdom in response to a question. He was on his way up to Jerusalem, where he would offer his life as the atoning blood sacrifice for our sins. He was traveling from town to town, preaching the gospel and proclaiming (as he often did) that the kingdom was near, when someone in the crowd stopped him to ask a theological question: "Lord, will those who are saved be few?" (Luke 13:23).

This is a question people still ask today. How wide is God's mercy? Will most people make it into his kingdom, or only some people? How many will be saved, and how many lost?

This question may have been prompted by some of the things that Jesus said about the way of salvation. To give one notable example, in the Sermon on the Mount he said: "Enter by the narrow gate. For the gate is wide and the way is easy that leads to destruction, and those who enter by it are many. For the gate is narrow and the way is hard that leads to life, and those who find it are few" (Matt. 7:13–14).

This is what Jesus said. But other people were talking about this issue, too. It was a common point of theological conversation in those days—the kind of topic that synagogue students discussed back in their dorm rooms, late at night. Everyone knew that some people would be redeemed, while others would be damned. What they wondered about was the relative proportions. As they considered the love and the justice of God, they wondered how many souls would be saved, and how many lost.

Back then it was commonly believed that not many people would be saved at all. The people of Israel would be saved, of course. According to the rabbinic writings, "All Israelites have a share in the world to come."[1] But apart from a few rare exceptions, the Gentiles would be lost forever. So relatively few people would be saved. This was the conventional wisdom.

But what did Jesus think? Here is the surprising answer he gave:

> Strive to enter in through the narrow door. For many, I tell you, will seek to enter and will not be able. When once the master of the house has risen and shut the door, and you begin to stand outside and to knock at the door, saying, "Lord, open to us," then he will answer you, "I do not know where you come from." Then you will begin to say, "We ate and drank in your presence, and you taught in our streets." But he will say, "I tell you, I do not know where you come from. Depart from me, all you workers of evil!" In that place there will be weeping and gnashing of teeth, when you see Abraham and Isaac and Jacob and all the prophets in the kingdom of God but you yourselves cast out. And people will come from east and west, and from north and south, and recline at table in the kingdom of God. And behold, some are last who will be first, and some are first who will be last. (Luke 13:24–30)

In the history of the world, no one has ever given better answers to questions that Jesus did. In this case, he pulled a matter of theological speculation—the many and the few—down to the level of personal application. Cyril of Alexandria explained it like this: Jesus is "purposely silent to the useless question" but "proceeds to speak of what was essential"—namely, the salvation of our souls.[2] How many people God will save is his business. The real question for us is whether *we* will be saved. It is a good question for everyone to ask: have I entered the narrow door that leads to eternal life? Do I know for sure that I will be saved?

Trying the Wrong Door

Jesus took the question of how many people would be saved and used it as a key to unlock the door of salvation. In his answer he mentions three different ways one can easily miss the kingdom of God. If we want to be sure not to miss out on the kingdom, it is important to listen to what he says.

Notice how Jesus begins his answer: "Strive to enter through the narrow door" (Luke 13:24). Here the Savior uses a word for intense exertion, like an athlete in training. It is the Greek term (*agonizesthe*) from which we derive the word "agonize." Jesus is not saying that we need to "sweat out" our salvation. But he *is* saying that we need to be intentional about eternal life. While it is true that we can never work our way to God, we do need to labor hard to understand the message of salvation. Until we have received the assurance of eternal life, we need to keep striving to understand the gospel. Many people miss the kingdom of God because they never give any serious attention to the destiny of their souls, and Jesus does not want us to be among them.

One way of missing the kingdom is by trying to enter at the wrong door. This is the implication of the exhortation in verse 24: "Strive to enter through the narrow door"—the door that leads to life. The image of the narrow door implies that fewer people than we expect will enter eternal life. Presumably the alternative is a broad door—or maybe many broad doors—all of which lead to destruction.

This way of thinking about faith is contrary to the prevailing views of our culture. The exclusivity of Christianity offends people. Today it is more common to think of the world's many religions as different doors that lead to the same destination. Eventually Christians, Buddhists, Muslims, and Hindus will all end up in the same kingdom. Religion is a personal preference that makes no ultimate difference. This kind of pluralism was clearly expressed by actor Chad Allen in a 2006 interview on CNN. When asked about his personal view of God, Allen said:

> I judge all my actions by my relationship with god of my understanding. It's very powerful, and it's taken its own shape and form. And I am very much at peace in the knowledge that in my heart God created this beautiful expression of my love. . . . It is a deep-founded, faith-based belief in god based upon the work that I've done growing up as a Catholic boy and then reaching out to Buddhist philosophy, to Hindu philosophy, to Native American beliefs and finally as I got through my course with addiction and alcoholism and finding a higher power that worked for me.[3]

This is not a view of God that finds any support in the teaching of Jesus Christ. How could it? Jesus is the one and only God-man, the unique Son of God, who has offered the only atonement for sin, and who alone has risen from the grave with the power of eternal life. Jesus shed his own blood to open the door. How could he ever say that there is any other entrance to the kingdom except through him? "I am the door," Jesus said. "If anyone enters by me, he will be saved" (John 10:9). Cecil Frances Alexander expressed this truth beautifully in a song she wrote for the boys and girls in her Sunday school class back in the 1840s: "There was no other good enough to pay the price of sin; he only could unlock the gate of heav'n and let us in."[4]

Insisting on entering the kingdom by another door is not merely bad theology; it is also bad manners. By way of illustration, imagine a visitor refusing to enter a private home because the front door is the only way in. The problem in such a case is not the door, but the visitor's attitude. Or consider a memorable scene in *The Magician's Nephew* by C. S. Lewis. The lion-king Aslan sends the boy Digory on a long journey into the mountains, to retrieve a life-giving apple from the garden at the top of a steep, green hill. When he reaches the garden, Digory finds that it is surrounded by walls and guarded by golden gates. On the gates, the following words of warning are written in silver: "Come in by the gold gates or not at all."

Digory wonders who would want to climb the wall, if all one has to do is enter by the gate. But once he picks the apple, he discovers that he is not alone. A witch has clambered over the wall to steal some of the fruit for herself. As soon as Digory sees her, he knows that she is not saved. The story of someone who chooses to climb a forbidden wall rather than to enter by an open door will end in despair.[5]

Jesus says the same thing will be true for everyone who chooses not to enter the door he opens to his eternal kingdom. That door is wide enough to save anyone who comes to him in repentance and faith. Rather than criticizing him for not opening other doors, therefore, or trying to force our way in someplace else, we should enter the one door that lets us enter in. Christianity is as narrow as the narrow door, but that door is wide enough to save anyone who enters.

Knocking Too Late

Furthermore, we should enter now, while we still have the time. The narrow door will not stay open forever. If the first way to miss the kingdom is by trying the wrong door, the second way to miss it is by knocking too late at the right door. Jesus said, "For many, I tell you, will seek to enter and will not be able. When once the master of the house has risen and shut the door, and you begin to stand outside and to knock at the door, saying, 'Lord, open to us,' then he will answer you, 'I do not know where you come from'" (Luke 13:24–25).

The picture here is of a homeowner who closes his door and then locks it for the night. All day long he has offered free and open hospitality. But when the darkness comes, and it is time to sleep, he will shut his door for the night.

It is clear from the wording of verse 25 that Jesus himself is the master of this house. He is telling us something important about how he operates the door to his kingdom. Earlier he described the door in spatial terms and told us that it is narrow. Here he describes it in temporal terms and tells us that it will not be open for long. Now the door is open, but soon it will be closed, never to open again. People wanted to know *how many* (how many people would get in), but Jesus wanted them to think about *how soon* (how soon the door would close for all eternity).

What makes these verses especially troubling is that they describe people who apparently want to get into the kingdom of God, and yet are denied access. Maybe they are too late, but at least they are seeking the kingdom. They call Jesus, "Lord." They knock at his door—the right door—and ask him to let them in. Yet, sadly, it is too late for them. For a long time the door was open, but now they are shut out.

Before we see why the door is shut, we need to make sure that we do not miss the practical application. The time to put our trust in Jesus Christ and start living for him is not sometime in the future, but right now. "It is appointed for man to die once," the Scripture says, "and after that comes judgment" (Heb. 9:27). People do not come back from death and then choose a different destiny. The life we have for making our kingdom choice is this life, and not the life to come. Our eternal state, said the Scottish theologian Thomas Boston, is determined by our relationship to Christ at the moment when death "will open the doors of heaven or hell" to us.[6]

Do not miss the kingdom by knocking too late on the door of salvation. When Billy Graham visited the campus of Wheaton College in 1976 he called his message "The Time Is Short." Here is the wise counsel he gave:

> It will someday be too late. It's very dangerous to come to a school like Wheaton if you're not sure you know Christ as your Lord and Savior. You will hear so much gospel here and so much Bible here that your heart will get harder and harder. God will continue to speak but your resistance will be greater. So accept Christ now. Don't wait. "Now is the accepted time. Today is the day of salvation!"[7]

Making Assumptions

Do you find it shocking that Jesus will shut the door on some people? If so, then realize that you are not the only one who is surprised. The people who get closed out will be even more shocked than we are. Remember, these are people who want to enter the kingdom. So why can't they get in? Is it just a matter of bad timing? And if so, then isn't God's refusal to let them in terribly arbitrary?

It is important to see that something deeper is at work here. There is a third way that people miss the kingdom, or perhaps a reason behind the second way. These people miss the kingdom because even though they have heard about Jesus, they do not really know him. They miss the kingdom because they do not have a personal relationship with Jesus Christ.

Here Jesus is talking about religious people who always assumed that they were part of his plan. Notice what they say to the master of the house. When Jesus tells them that he does not know who they are, they immediately come back with all kinds of objections. "We ate and drank in your presence," they say, "and you taught in our streets" (Luke 13:26). In other words, these are people who experienced Jesus firsthand. They knew him socially, and listened to him preach. They saw him perform miracles. But the one thing they never did was enter into a relationship with him of loving trust. They never asked him to forgive their sins, invited him to be their Savior, or worshiped him as their God.

This explains why they were so late to start knocking on the kingdom door. They should have been committed to Christ all along. But they never really knew him at all. So when they finally did come knocking on his door, he didn't know them, either.

The same thing happens today. Some people have an outward connection with Christianity as a religion without having a personal relationship with Christ as Lord. One of the most likely places for this to happen is on the campus of a Christian college or high school. Students call themselves Christians. They sign a statement that they will live the kind of life that Christians live. They go to Bible class and learn theology. They go to chapel as often as they are supposed to and listen to the message of the gospel. Yet no one ever gets saved simply by their proximity to Christianity. Salvation comes through personal faith in Jesus Christ. So students on Christian campuses—or even members of local churches—may identify in some way with Christianity without ever truly entering the kingdom of Jesus Christ.

Jesus wants us to know that for those who never ask his forgiveness, there will be eternal loss. One day he will say to them, "Depart from me, all you workers of evil!" (Luke 13:27). This is the clear and consistent teaching of Scripture. On another occasion Jesus told his disciples that when the day of judgment comes, "The Son of Man will send his angels, and they will gather out of his kingdom all causes of sin and all law-breakers, and throw them into the fiery furnace" (Matt. 13:41–42). We read the same thing in the rest of the New Testament, where kingdom language is used to describe the difference between the damned and the redeemed. "You may be sure of this," writes the apostle Paul, "that everyone who is sexually immoral or impure, or who is covetous (that is, an idolater), has no inheritance in the kingdom of Christ and God" (Eph. 5:5). The teaching of the New Testament could hardly be clearer: "The unrighteous will not inherit the kingdom of God" (1 Cor. 6:9; see Gal. 5:19–21).

Once Jesus shuts the kingdom door, it will stay shut, and those who are left out will go to a place of dreadful remorse, of "weeping and gnashing of teeth" (Luke 13:28). This is as much as we need to know about that awful place, because really the worst thing about hell is missing the kingdom. Who can imagine the loss of those who hear the gospel, but reject it? They will never sit down to the everlasting banquet that Jesus promises, when his people come from north and west and east and south to feast in the kingdom of God. Although they were on the guest list, they declined God's free invitation. So instead of sitting down to the feast, they will be separated from God, separated from his Son, and separated from his loving Spirit forever. David Gooding writes: "To have been so near to Christ on earth without receiving him and without coming to know him personally, and therefore to be shut out for ever from the glorious company of the saints, while others from distant times and cultures have found the way in—who shall measure the disappointment and frustration of it?"[8]

The Final Reversal

This passage ends with a famous verse that is rarely considered in its proper context. Understand that when Jesus said "the last will be first, and the first will be last" (Luke 13:30) he was not giving us a punch line to use outside the dining hall, or at the roller coaster, or wherever long lines are found; Jesus was stating a serious principle of salvation. We will be very surprised to learn who makes it into the kingdom. Some people we were sure would make it never will. They will end up outside, looking in. But some people will be there that we never expected—people from everywhere, broken-down people who never seemed to have anything going for them. But they did know Jesus, and Jesus knew them, which in the end is what matters more than anything else in the world.

Jesus tells us to strive to enter by the narrow door. Salvation is a limited-time offer. No gospel will be preached in hell. By then it will be too late to repent, too late to believe, and too late to enter the kingdom of God. So the question is not how many doors there are. God knows there is only one. The question is whether we will enter the one and only door while we still have the time. Don't miss the kingdom of God!

6

Proclaiming the Kingdom

In the broken ruins of a bombed-out city, one man performed a solitary act of musical courage. It happened in the 1990s, when the Bosnian War was ravaging the city of Sarajevo. There were deadly snipers on the nearby hillsides. Every night bombs destroyed shops and homes and civic buildings. Desperate citizens scurried between the piles of rubble, looking for cover as they foraged for bread—the victims of war.

One explosion was especially deadly. A bomb fell directly on a group of people lined up outside a bakery, hoping to get a morsel of bread when it opened for business. The blast killed all twenty-two of them.

The next day Vedran Smajlovic came to the scene. He set up a chair, carefully removed his cello from its case, and began to play the beautiful strains of Albinoni's *Ada-*

gio. He did the same thing the next day, and the day after that—twenty-two adagios for twenty-two victims.

"The Cellist of Sarajevo," they began to call him. As a veteran of the Sarajevo Philharmonic Orchestra, he would not let his music be silenced. Nor would he let his people's hope grow dim. So Smajlovic played for funerals. He performed solo concerts in bombed-out buildings. In a place of death and destruction, his cello became an instrument of hope and his life a witness to holy beauty.[1]

Like the Cellist of Sarajevo, we have a melody to play. We live in the broken ruins of a fallen world, where death and pain are daily realities. Yet as followers of Christ we do not lose hope. Instead, we scrape out the gospel on the strings of our souls, making music that proclaims the coming of the kingdom of God.

How It Started

We believe in kingdom come. This is not the last and final world. The kingdom is near, as Jesus promised. He is coming soon, and when he does, he will make all things new. So we live in the hopeful expectation of the kingdom of God.

Yet we also know that many people are in danger of missing that happy kingdom. Jesus said that the door is narrow, and that soon it will be shut forever. This ought to give us a sense of urgency—not just about our own salvation, but also about sharing the gospel with others. Some people are still outside, and part of our calling as

Christians is to invite them to come in. So, rather than doubting the reality of the coming judgment, or disagreeing with God about how wide the door ought to be, we should proclaim his kingdom everywhere, to everyone, for as long as we can.

The church has had this calling since the very day that Jesus ascended to heaven. We see this clearly in the opening verses of Acts. After he rose from the grave, Jesus remained on this earth for forty days. During that time he gave his disciples their final course in the gospel. He taught them the same thing he had taught them from the very beginning of his ministry: the kingdom of God.

Jesus had begun his public ministry by preaching the good news and saying, "The kingdom is near." He continued to do this all the way through to the end of his ministry. Jesus went through Galilee, and then through all the towns in Israel, "teaching in their synagogues and proclaiming the gospel of the kingdom" (Matt. 4:23; 9:35). It was not just the gospel that Jesus preached, but specifically the gospel *of the kingdom*. He was always "proclaiming and bringing the good news of the kingdom of God" (Luke 8:1). In doing so, Jesus was putting the good news in the cosmic context of God's sovereign rule. He even did this on the cross, when he promised that one of the thieves who died next to him would come into his kingdom (Luke 23:42–43).

Proclaiming the kingdom was central to the life mission of Jesus Christ. We should not be surprised, therefore, that at the beginning of Acts Jesus presented himself to his disciples and spoke with them "about the kingdom of God" (Acts 1:3). If you have ever wondered what Jesus said to his disciples after he rose from the dead, this is it. The risen Christ preached the kingdom of God.

These sermons raised a question in the minds of the disciples. (Just think how much less we would know about Jesus without the disciples and all their questions!) It was a question they had asked before. It seemed to come up almost every time that Jesus proclaimed the kingdom—a question of timing. Jesus said the kingdom was near. Well, how near was it? People ask the same question today. Here is how the disciples put it: "Lord, will you at this time restore the kingdom to Israel?" (Acts 1:6).

By now we know better than to expect Jesus to answer this kind of question directly. Like a master in the art of judo, he knew how to absorb a question and throw its weight in a different direction—the direction someone ought to be going. That is what he does here. Jesus does not want us to speculate about the kingdom's timing. Instead, he wants us to concentrate on proclaiming its gospel. So he said: "It is not for you to know times or seasons that the Father has fixed by his own authority. But you will receive power when the Holy Spirit has come upon you, and you will be my witnesses in Jerusalem and in all Judea and Samaria, and to the end of the earth" (Acts 1:7–8).

With these words, Jesus ascended to heaven in a cloud of glory, and the great missionary work of the church began.

The command to bear witness was for the original apostles, but it was not for them alone. This calling is for the whole body of Christ, right up to the present time. Eric Liddell, the famous Olympic gold medalist and missionary to China, said, "We are all missionaries. Wherever we go, we either bring people nearer to Christ, or we repel them from Christ. We are working for the great Kingdom of God."[2]

So proclaim the kingdom of Jesus Christ. Proclaim it everywhere, until the end of the world, when Jesus comes again and his kingdom rules over all.

Proclaim the Kingdom

First, proclaim the kingdom. This is not always the verb we use when we talk about the kingdom of Jesus Christ. We often talk about building the kingdom, or advancing the kingdom, or working for the kingdom. But the verb that the Bible typically uses is "proclaim." The kingdom of God is not primarily an action we perform, but a message we proclaim. The kingdom mainly comes by preaching.

The book of Acts provides many examples of the apostles preaching the kingdom of God. Jesus called these men to be his witnesses, and they fulfilled this calling by proclaiming the gospel. Every one of their sermons—whether of Peter, Stephen, Philip, or Paul—proclaims that Jesus died for our sins and rose again. They were always preaching the crucifixion and the resurrection—in other words, the gospel.

But their witness is also defined as proclaiming the kingdom. For example, when Paul went to Ephesus, the Bible says that he was "reasoning and persuading them about the kingdom of God" (Acts 19:8). This is the same thing that Paul did everywhere. Thus he described his ministry as one of "proclaiming the kingdom" (Acts 20:25). In seeing the risen Christ, Paul and the other apostles had witnessed the coming of the kingdom of God. And, as the Dutch theologian Herman Ridderbos explains in his masterful book *The Coming of the Kingdom*, the coming of the kingdom enables the gospel itself to operate "with an entirely new force, and an intensified content; it is the preaching of the fulfillment; it is the message of the grace of God revealed in Christ which now starts its course in this world."[3]

To proclaim the kingdom is to announce—not simply through God-honoring actions, but especially through gospel-communicating words—that Jesus Christ is Savior and Lord. It is to tell people that he is the Creator God who lived for us, died for us, and rose again for us with the power of eternal life. It is to declare that this Jesus is now the supreme ruler of the universe—that all things in heaven and earth are under his authority. And it is to invite people to come into his blessed kingdom by surrendering to his gracious rule.

A helpful, biblically faithful definition of evangelism comes from the Lausanne Covenant of 1974:

> To evangelize is to spread the good news that Jesus Christ died for our sins and was raised from the dead according

to the Scriptures, and that as the reigning Lord he now offers the forgiveness of sins and the liberating gift of the Spirit to all who repent and believe. Our Christian presence in the world is indispensable to evangelism, and so is that kind of dialogue whose purpose is to listen sensitively in order to understand. But evangelism itself is the proclamation of the historical, biblical Christ as Saviour and Lord, with a view to persuading people to come to him personally and so be reconciled to God.

Each of us has a part to play in proclaiming the gospel. The Holy Spirit does not outsource evangelism; he calls *us* to do it. Yet many of us come up with excuses for not sharing our faith. We say that we do not have any good opportunities, or that we do not have the gift of evangelism. But maybe the real problem is that we do not trust the Holy Spirit to do what he has promised and use God's Word to bring people to faith in Christ—not always because of our efforts, but sometimes in spite of them.

Be careful not to make proclaiming the kingdom more complicated than it really is. Sometimes it is as easy as inviting someone to church. A simple example comes from the witness of Becky Wilson, who works in the admissions department at Wheaton College. At a local park she saw a Chinese woman looking after her daughter. They struck up a conversation, and before long Becky invited the woman to do something that as an atheist she had never done before: read the Bible.

The woman studied the Bible with Becky for a while,

first at a Backyard Bible Club for children, and then at a women's Bible study. Eventually she decided she didn't want to get up so early in the morning, so she started to attend an evening Bible study. What Becky will never forget is the look of overwhelming joy on her friend's face the day she came running up in the parking lot after school to announce that she had given her life to Christ. It had happened the night before, when she read what Jesus said about loving your enemies, which she knew she could never do—only God.

The woman went home and asked her husband for permission to become a Christian. He said yes because he had met some of her Christian friends and could see how much she was changing for the better. The woman stayed up all night reading her Bible. She kept reading all morning, and all afternoon. When she told Becky about it, she said, "It is like I have new eyes! It is like everything is in color now when it was colorless before!"

Have you ever experienced the stunning joy of helping someone see the world in gospel color? God is able to use our witness to bring someone into the kingdom of God. But we need to be intentional about sharing the good news. Are you involved in one ministry that teaches people the gospel? Is there one person you are praying will come to faith in Christ? Are you ready for one opportunity to tell someone that Jesus died on the cross to pay for their sins and rose again to give them eternal life?

When the time is right, your words will be a life-saving

witness. David Horner teaches philosophy and apologetics at Biola University. In his book *Mind Your Faith*, he describes a conversation he had when he was a university student. A freshman from the debate team came up and said, "Are you Dave Horner? I hear you're a Christian." When Horner admitted that he was, the debater proceeded to ask a challenging question, "What's a Christian?"

Anticipating an argument, Horner tried to come up with an airtight definition of Christianity, using as many theological distinctions as possible. Yet as the conversation continued, he began to sense that he was taking the wrong approach. "Wait a minute," he said, "are you asking me what a Christian is because you want to *become* a Christian?" When the student said yes, Horner took him outside for a long conversation that ended with him praying to receive Christ.[4] When the time is right, the Holy Spirit will use us to bring someone into the kingdom of God. We only need to be ready when the time comes.

Proclaim It Everywhere

The calling to proclaim the gospel is something we carry with us wherever we go. When Jesus told the apostles to be his witnesses, he told them to start right where they were, in Jerusalem. But he also sent them out to Judea, Samaria, and the ends of the earth. The way Paul describes this to the Romans is thrilling. He says that by the power of the Holy Spirit, he had proclaimed the gospel of Jesus Christ "from Jerusalem and all the way around to Illyricum" (Rom. 15:19). In other words, he had preached the gospel across the Mediterranean world.

This is our calling as well: to proclaim the kingdom everywhere. The gospel is intended to go *from* every place, *to* every place. Strictly speaking, from the perspective of Acts chapter 1 most of us live at "the end of the earth," not in Jerusalem, Judea, or Samaria. But many Christians have taken the command that Jesus gave his disciples as the pattern for all Christians everywhere. Wherever we are—this place is our Jerusalem. No one else in the world is in a better position than we are to reach the people within our own network of relationships.

Our proclamation of the gospel does not stop here, however. As kingdom-minded Christians, we are called to have a wider concern for the work of the gospel around the world, and to do our part in supporting that work. No one has described this calling with greater passion than the great London preacher Charles Spurgeon:

> The Christian church was designed from the first to be aggressive. It was not intended to remain stationary at any period, but to advance onward until its boundaries became commensurate with those of the world. It was not intended to radiate from one point only; but to form numerous centers from which its influence might spread to the surrounding parts.[5]

Wheaton College is one of those numerous centers for evangelism. Very possibly, Wheaton alums have preached the gospel to more people than any other Christian community in the history of the world. Of course, given the fact that Billy Graham is one of its graduates, this is hardly a fair comparison! It is estimated that over the course of his lifetime, through various evangelistic campaigns and media broadcasts, Dr. Graham has preached the gospel to more than three hundred million people in almost two hundred countries.

He is not the only one. I think of many other Wheaton alumni—ordinary people who have shared the gospel in extraordinary ways. I think of Torrey Johnson, who made his decision for Christ in Pierce Chapel and went on to found Youth for Christ. I think of Robert Evans, who founded Greater Europe Mission. I think of Rodger Lewis and his wife Leila. Students who knew them in the 1940s remember the little song that Rodger used to sing: "Some may want to live within the sound of chimes or church bell; I want to run a rescue shop within a yard of hell." Rodger and Leila went on to become missionaries to Indonesia for more than forty years.

Then I think of my own personal friends. I think of Howard Blair, who planted a church in Japan that became a missionary-sending church. Or of Don "Bubba" Church, who was one of the first Christian coaches to take athletes behind the Iron Curtain. Or of Doug Birdsall, who led the Lausanne Congress on World Evangelization in Cape Town. I think of my classmates Thomas and Susanna Smoak, who share the gospel with street children in Sao Paulo. And

I think of the work that two former Wheaton football players are doing in Kansas City—Kevin Cawley and Kris McGee. Three years after planting a church in the heart of Kansas City's nightlife district, they had more than a thousand worshipers—many of them new converts—coming to hear the straightforward proclamation of biblical truth.

I mention these examples not to celebrate Wheaton College, which is only one small example of God's work in the world, but to challenge you to consider where *you* will proclaim the gospel. Evangelism is the original form of viral marketing. One person shares the gospel with another person, who shares it with someone else. God's strategy for the evangelization of the world is contagious Christians who carry the gospel wherever they go. This will never work if all we catch is a mild case of Christianity. But if we come down with full-blown faith in Jesus Christ, God can use our words of gospel truth—confirmed by deeds of Christlike love—to bring people into his kingdom.

Until the End of the World

We are called to keep witnessing for Christ until the end of the world. We proclaim the gospel of the kingdom. We proclaim it everywhere. And we keep on proclaiming it until Jesus comes again.

We get a hint of this calling at the beginning of Acts, after Jesus ascended to his Father, when the angel told the disciples to stop looking up into heaven. Instead, they were supposed to go out and do what Jesus told them to do, which was to proclaim the gospel. They were to do this in light of the fact that one day Jesus would come again, just the way he left, on clouds of glory (Acts 1:11). The implication is that until Jesus does come again, we should stay busy proclaiming the gospel.

The apostle Paul is a perfect example. The last chapter of Acts tells the story of his final witness to Rome, where he was "testifying to the kingdom" (Acts 28:23). Even after they put him under house arrest, he kept preaching the gospel to anyone who would come to listen. He kept "proclaiming the kingdom of God and teaching about the Lord Jesus Christ with all boldness and without hindrance" (v. 31). I hope that's what people find me doing when the end finally comes: sharing the kingdom of God.

Nearly every time that the New Testament talks about the coming of the kingdom of God, it makes the same practical application: we should keep sharing the gospel while we still have the time. We see this perhaps most clearly near the end of Matthew, where Jesus talks about the end of the age. He said to his disciples, "This gospel of the kingdom will be proclaimed throughout the whole world as a testimony to all nations, and then the end will come" (Matt. 24:14).

This promise puts evangelism into eschatological perspective. Jesus ties our proclaiming of the kingdom to his coming with the kingdom. The end is closer than ever before. Jesus did not say exactly what counts as proclaiming the gospel to a nation. Nor did he promise that the end would come immediately after the last person on earth that needs to hear the gospel does hear the gospel. But we live at a time when missionaries are planning to go to the last unreached people groups and translate the Bible into the last known languages. Some missionary leaders believe we are only a decade or two away from fulfilling the Great Commission.

This possibility leads Leith Anderson to believe that we are living at one of the most exciting times in history. We sometimes imagine that in heaven there will be long lines of people waiting to meet the apostle Paul or listen to Peter tell stories about Jesus. But maybe those great men will be just as eager to speak with the world's last evangelists—the people who completed their task of carrying the gospel to the ends of the earth. They will ask, "What was it like to live in that moment of history when the work begun in the first century was finally completed, and all on Earth had the opportunity to hear the Gospel?"[6]

What is your part in that great story? Maybe it will only be a small part. But if it is, then know this: no kingdom work is so small that it is not worth doing as well as you can do it. Sometimes we get overwhelmed by the needs of the world, and all the gospel work that needs to be done. Don't get discouraged, and don't feel like you have to respond to every gospel cause. Rejoice in what other Christians are doing—whatever God has called them to do. Then pray for the courage and the faithfulness to do the one thing that God calls you to do—whatever that is. Tell him that your life is totally open to his plan, and that even if you have never led anyone to Christ, or done a credible job of sharing the gospel, you are willing to proclaim the good news.

Then keep proclaiming the kingdom all the way to the end of your life, or until Jesus comes again—whichever comes first. During his travels to America, George White-field contracted a high fever. Desperately ill, and feeling somewhat sorry for himself, the famous evangelist believed that he was dying. But the black woman who served as his nursemaid said, "No, master Whitefield, you are not to die yet; there are thousands of souls to bring to Christ, so keep up your spirits, for you must live, and not die."[7]

As long as there is life in us, we should never give up hope. In the ruins of a fallen world, we should pull out our gospel cello and keep playing the melody of salvation as we proclaim the kingdom of God.

7

When the Kingdom Doesn't Come

If we believe in Christ, then we believe in his kingdom. We believe that God has a plan for this world—a plan to rescue it and redeem it. We believe that someday soon Christ will come again, and that when he does, he will set everything straight. We also believe that in many ways his kingdom is already coming. Because of the death and resurrection of Jesus, and by the power of the Holy Spirit, wherever the gospel is proclaimed, his kingdom comes.

But what do you do when the kingdom *doesn't* come? Wherever we go, we meet people whose lives are shattered by sin. The more we know about the world, the more deeply we feel the pain of its brokenness. Communities are stuck in cycles of poverty they are powerless to escape. Orphans grow up without ever knowing the love of a mother or father. Little girls are sold into sexual slavery. People with curable conditions die for lack of basic medical care. Even when we pray, the kingdom doesn't always come.

So what do you do when the kingdom doesn't come in your own life, at least as far as you can see? What do you do when the doubts grow, when the emptiness refuses to go away, when you are betrayed by a friend, when sin has you in its grip and won't let go, when relationships are wounded by prejudice, or when a secret evil is discovered? What do you do when the kingdom doesn't come?

The Servants' Test

Jesus gave one answer to this question near the end of his earthly ministry. Some Bible scholars are troubled by the fact that although the New Testament says that Jesus is coming soon, he still hasn't come. They treat the delay of the kingdom as some sort of biblical problem. This certainly wasn't a problem for Jesus, however.

He knew there would be a gap between the now and the not yet, between the present and the future reality of the kingdom of God. Even before he died and rose again, Jesus told his disciples that there would be a delay between his first and second comings, between his departure and his return.

This is one of the great questions of our lives, too, and one of the most important tests of our discipleship. As we wait for the kingdom to come, are we living as faithful servants of the once and future King? The delay between his departure and his return reveals our true commitment to Christ.

Jesus helped his disciples prepare for this delay the same way that he prepared them for a lot of things—by telling them a story: "As they heard these things, he proceeded to tell a parable, because he was near to Jerusalem, and because they supposed that the kingdom of God was to appear immediately" (Luke 19:11). In fact, the kingdom of God would *not* appear immediately—not in all its fullness. So Jesus told us a story that would help us know what to do in the meantime.

We need to listen carefully, because this particular parable is similar to other stories that Jesus told, but different. In this story, there are two groups of people who wait for the return of a king: his former servants and his future subjects. One commentator summarizes the story like this: "The King would return only after an unspecified, but far from negligible, period of time; and during that time, though his enemies might be plotting against him, he would expect his servants to be laboring to establish his kingdom."[1]

Some of the citizens who waited for the nobleman's return were enemies to his cause—out-and-out rebels who rejected the kingship of the king. Many people had the same attitude about Jesus as he made his way to the cross. They refused to acknowledge him as their rightful king. Soon they would call for his crucifixion and say, "We have no king but Caesar" (John 19:15).

We will learn what happened to those rebels at the end of the story. But the parable focuses more on the king's servants. There were ten of them in all, and each was given a mina to manage in the king's absence. This coin, which was worth about three months' wages, was large enough to test whether these servants could be trusted to serve their master. He said to them, "Engage in business until I come" (Luke 19:13). The servants were called to get busy for their master, putting his money to work.

These ten money managers represent the servants of Christ, the King. As we wait for his royal return, we are called to carry out the spiritual business of his kingdom. But what, exactly, does the money represent?

It is important to recognize an important difference between this parable in Luke and a similar parable in Matthew. Matthew says nothing about a king, but only about a man who went on a long journey (Matt. 25:14). Each of that man's servants received a different amount of money, depending on his ability (v. 15). Thus, Matthew's parable indicates that we all have different talents to use in serving the Lord.

In Luke each servant receives the *same* amount of money: one mina per servant (Luke 19:13). While it is true that we all have different gifts, that is not the point of this parable. This one is more about faithfulness than giftedness: every believer has the same responsibility to work for the kingdom until Jesus comes again.

We have all received the same gospel, and Jesus wants

us to put it to work. The gospel is simply the good news of God's grace. It is the message of salvation through the death and resurrection of Jesus Christ. It is the royal offer of forgiveness through the cross and eternal life through the empty tomb. God has invested this good news in us, and now he wants us to multiply his spiritual capital, yielding a good return for the gospel.

This investment opportunity raises some important questions: How am I putting the gospel to work? What profit will I have to show when Jesus comes again? What will I do with the gospel this month, next month, and for the rest of my life?

There are all kinds of ways to put the gospel to work. We do it most of all by believing that what the gospel says about us is true: we are accepted in Christ. Therefore, our significance is not determined by our grade in chemistry, by racing the fastest time at our distance, by the chair we sit in when we play our violin in the orchestra, by our sales performance over the last quarter, by the number of friends we have in cyberspace, or by anything else except the grace that God has for us in Jesus Christ.

Then we put the gospel to use by living out its implications. This means staying committed to our calling so God can use us in someone else's life. It means not giving up on a difficult relationship, but having the hard conversation that the Holy Spirit can use to bring reconciliation. It means turning toward God with our doubts, not away from him. It means that as we look to the future, we surrender our lives again to the plan that God has for us, even if it's not the plan that we have for us. These are all gospel ways of living for Jesus.

The King's Return

One day the king will return, and when he does, one of the first things he will want to know is which servants he can trust, based on what we did in his absence. When the master returned with his kingdom, "he ordered these servants to whom he had given the money to be called to him, that he might know what they had gained by doing business" (Luke 19:15). The day of return was a day of reckoning, on which the king rightly demanded the fruit of faithful service.

Two of the servants made good on the king's investment, at varying rates of return: "The first came before him, saying, 'Lord, your mina has made ten minas more.' And he said to him, 'Well done, good servant! Because you have been faithful in a very little, you shall have authority over ten cities.' And the second came, saying, 'Lord, your mina has made five minas.' And he said to him, 'And you are to be over five cities'" (vv. 16–19). These were excellent rates of return. Anyone who can turn a profit of five hundred or a thousand percent knows how to manage other people's money!

Jesus partly told this parable to help us understand God's economy—the business of the kingdom. Notice that the gospel grows by its inherent power. When the servants were asked what they had done with what they had, they made it sound like the money had grown all by itself. "Lord, your mina has made ten minas more," they said (v. 16), or "your mina has made five minas" (v. 18). These servants did not boast about what they had done, but credited their profit to what the master had given them. It was the mina that made the increase.

So it is with the gospel. God tells us to put the gospel to work, and because it is the power of God unto salvation, that very gospel makes the kingdom grow. It is amazing what the good news can do! It delivers people from their bondage to sin, turning God's enemies into friends. It brings people from death to life and makes them the sons and the daughters of God. Then it sends people out into the world with the love of Jesus Christ, to serve and to sacrifice.

When I think of the power of the gospel, I think of a friend from Philadelphia who came to faith in Christ through a gospel tract that stuck to the bottom of his shoe. He pulled it off, glanced at it, and tossed it aside. But later he picked it up, read it, and gave his life to Jesus Christ. Or I think of a man from the old Soviet Union. As he was reading communist attacks on Christianity, he was more and more intrigued by the Bible. So he began copying down the Bible verses that these writings would quote as part of their attack, in effect making his own little Bible. What he read in those scattered Bible verses was enough to bring him to Christ. Eventually, he traveled to the nearest city, went to a large park, and prayed that God would bring him into contact with another Christian, which of course is exactly what happened.

When we see what the gospel has done, not just in the lives of other people, but also in our own lives, we know that none of the credit goes to us. It all goes to God, because his gospel is what makes things grow.

The parable of the minas teaches us further that when our King comes again, he will hold us accountable for what we have done with what we have. As the Scripture says, "We must all appear before the judgment seat of Christ, so that each one may receive what is due for what he has done" (2 Cor. 5:10). In the very last chapter of the Bible, Jesus said, "Behold, I am coming soon, bringing my recompense with me, to repay each one for what he has done" (Rev. 22:12).

So let me ask, in the expectation of eternity: What are you doing with what you have? Jesus is watching and waiting to see whether we can be trusted. What we do with our lives—what we do with the gospel—has eternal significance. Hudson Taylor was right when he said, "A little thing is just a little thing, but faithfulness in a little thing is a great thing." The truth of that statement will be confirmed when the kingdom comes, and all the little things that people do with the gospel will receive their great reward.

The Wicked Servant's Loss

Sadly, there was one servant who failed to serve the king, and this parable is about him too: "Then another came, saying, 'Lord, here is your mina, which I kept laid away in a handkerchief; for I was afraid of you'" (Luke 19:20–21).

What this servant did—or failed to do—was shocking. In complete defiance of the instructions he was given, he wrapped his treasure in a handkerchief, hid it under his mattress, and waited for his master to return. Rather than putting his money to good use, this unprofitable servant refused to use the gift that he was given. The other servants were entrepreneurs; if they had some money, they tried to get more. But this man was so afraid of what he might lose that he failed to work for what he could gain.

Some people do the same thing with the gifts that come from God. Rather than putting the gospel to good use, they are afraid to talk about their faith or to do anything else for Jesus that goes beyond their own abilities and therefore forces them to trust in the power of the Holy Spirit. Yet holding back from the call of God is not humility; it is pride and rebellion and fear.

Notice that rather than owning up to his failure, the third servant tried to blame his master. "I was afraid of you," he said, "because you are a severe man. You take what you did not deposit, and reap what you did not sow" (Luke 19:21). It wasn't *his* fault for being afraid; it was the king's fault for frightening him! Even if he made some extra money, the king would just take it away, so why bother? This was the unprofitable servant's thinking.

Some people have the same attitude toward God. They see him as a harsh taskmaster, who never gives but only takes, and never donates, only demands. The truth is that God has given us everything we have, including the very air that we breathe. Furthermore, when we go to the cross, we see that he has done everything that needed to be done for our salvation. Therefore, anything he demands from us is only a small return on what we have already received.

The servant's misrepresentation of his master—like our own unworthy thoughts about God—is contradicted by the rest of the parable. The master was not stingy; he was generous. But just for the sake of argument, the king granted his servant's premise: "He said to him, 'I will condemn you with your own words, you wicked servant! You knew that I was a severe man, taking what I did not deposit and reaping what I did not sow? Why then did you not put my money in the bank, and at my coming I might have collected it with interest?'" (Luke 19:22–23).

Even on his own terms, the servant should have done better. If what he said about his master was true, then at the very least he should have made a deposit in the bank. Do you see how wicked the man was? For that is how Jesus described him: "you wicked servant." Really, what else can anyone call a servant who refused to obey his master's command, slandered his master's good name, and was so scared of making a mistake that he failed to do what he could?

This is a sober warning for every Christian to consider. Understand that it is sinful not to use what we have in the service of God, to the best of our ability.

Use It or Lose It

As a wise investor, Jesus will put his gifts where they will get the most use. This is clear from the end of the parable, where the newly crowned king says, "Take the mina from him, and give it to the one who has the ten minas" (Luke 19:24). All the man wanted to do was keep what he had, but even that was taken away from him. This was a clear case of "use it or lose it."

Immediately, the other servants raised the obvious objection, "And they said to him, 'Lord, he has ten minas!'" (v. 25). In other words, that's not fair! Why should someone who has so much get even more, while someone who has next to nothing loses what little he has? The king responded by saying, "I tell you that to everyone who has, more will be given, but from the one who has not, even what he has will be taken away" (v. 26).

This is a hard saying. Yet from the standpoint of good business, this was the obvious thing to do. In fact, if you had the king's money, you would have done exactly the same thing. Capital should be invested with someone who has proven ability to make it grow, rather than risking it all on someone who is bankrupt.

As a shrewd investor, Jesus takes the same approach to ministry. He has entrusted us with the gospel, and now he wants us to be venture capitalists, spiritually speaking. If we handle his investment well, he will give us even more good work to do for the kingdom of God. The person who has, and uses it well, will get even more. But if we refuse to do anything for Jesus at all—well, what should he do?

People wonder whether the third servant was saved, or whether he was lost forever. The story never says. Maybe the wicked servant stands for someone who is in the church but does not actually have a saving relationship with Jesus Christ. J. C. Ryle thus describes him as a "professing Christian who is content with the idle possession of Christianity, and makes no effort to use it for his soul's good, or the glory of God."[2] The man is "wicked," after all, and he does lose the gospel, or at least the opportunity to use it for the King. He has no love for his master, and his service is so unfaithful that he fails to bear any fruit.

So perhaps the third servant is not a believer after all. However, Luke's parable is different from the one in Matthew, where the worthless servant is thrown into "the outer darkness" (Matt. 25:30). Furthermore, in Luke's gospel there may be a distinction between the wicked servant and the out-and-out enemies of the king who meet an even more terrible fate: "But as for these enemies of mine," said the king, "who did not want me to reign over them, bring them here and slaughter them before me" (Luke 19:27). This clearly refers to the final judgment and the damnation of God's enemies. On the day of his royal return, Christ the King will destroy every traitor to his cause and every rebel against his kingdom. The Bible says that Jesus will be "revealed from heaven with his mighty angels in flaming fire, inflicting vengeance on those who do not know God and on those who do not obey the gospel of our Lord Jesus. They will suffer the punishment of eternal destruction, away from the presence of the Lord and from the glory of his might" (2 Thess. 1:7–9).

Since the wicked servant is not explicitly included with the king's enemies—the ones who get slaughtered—then maybe he managed to escape their horrible fate. Perhaps he represents a fearful believer who does almost nothing for God, but still has some faith in Christ and thus barely gets saved. Yet his case seems far from hopeful, his salvation far from secure. Paralyzed by fear, and motivated only by his own self-preservation, he never did anything courageous for the kingdom of God.

Doing Something for Jesus

The question for us, of course, is not what happened to the man in the parable, but what will happen to us. The answer depends on what we do with what we have.

The Master has been gone a long time. We see so many troubles in the world that sometimes we wonder whether he will ever return. But we have a promise that one day soon Jesus will come again, in royal triumph. So I ask again: Are you working hard for his kingdom? Are you making wise investments with your time and talent that will strengthen your spiritual portfolio?

As I ask myself what I am doing with the gospel, I have to admit that I have done very little for Jesus, especially when I compare it to how much he has done for me. Maybe you have done more than I have; maybe you have done less. But whatever you have done with what you have, how could it ever be enough for Jesus? Even William Carey—the famous pioneer missionary to India—wrote his son a letter that said, "I am this day 58, but how little I have done for God."[3]

William Carey didn't stop there, however. Actually, what he had done for God was more than most people do. But even if it *was* only a little bit, the thing for him to do was to go out that day and do something for God, and then go out the next day and do something more. This is exactly what William Carey did. He kept serving the Lord until he died at the ripe old age of seventy-two. We should do the same thing. However much time we have, we should spend it all for Jesus.

After an extended mission trip to Peru, one Wheaton College student testified to the helplessness she felt as she watched her friend Jose Luis suffer the deprivations of urban poverty. She admitted it was tempting to say, "Don't worry, one day Jesus will take care of it. What can we really do about it now?" Yet she believed that she was called to something more. Her words call us to live and serve in hope, even when the kingdom doesn't come.

> I choose a different hope. I choose to believe in the resurrection. I choose to believe that in the grief, when I cannot see much hope at all, God is reconciling all things to himself. I choose to believe he does give us

small glimpses of his future kingdom where relationships among humanity and with his good creation will
be perfectly restored. It is this hope that allows me to
grieve over that which is utterly broken and yet not fall
into despair. . . . We have a response. We must live as
agents of God's redemption through his life-giving resurrection. Even when we can't always see it, we must
choose hope.[4]

8

When the Kingdom Comes

Sometimes you wait so long for something that you start to wonder if it will ever happen. You pound on the bottom of the bottle, but the ketchup insists on defying the laws of gravity. Your favorite team hasn't won a championship in more than a century, and the experts think they'll be lucky to win half their games this season. You thought you had a great interview, but it's been weeks since you heard anything; will you ever get a job?

Then, all of a sudden, it happens! The phone rings: they want you to start next week. Your team squeaks into the playoffs, gets hot in the postseason, and wins it all. With one glorious "blurp," gravity triumphs and your burger gets smothered in ketchup. Sometimes . . . after all the waiting . . . finally . . . it happens.

The kingdom of God is like that. It seems like we have

been waiting for it since forever. Ever since the first man and the first woman committed the first sin, we have been waiting for God to come and make things right again. Abraham, Moses, David, Elijah, Isaiah—they were all waiting for the kingdom.

Then Jesus came, and the kingdom was closer than ever. In a sense, it had already come, because Jesus is the King, and where the King is, the kingdom is. But Jesus also said that his dominion had not yet come in its full and final glory. The kingdom is at hand, he said. The kingdom is near. The kingdom is coming very soon.

Then, one day, all of a sudden, the promise will come true. The kingdom will not just be near, but actually here! We have God's word on it. Almost before we know it, Jesus will be here again. So many of the biblical prophecies about the second coming emphasize the suddenness of his appearance. It will happen "in a moment," the Scripture says, "in the twinkling of an eye" (1 Cor. 15:52). The day of the Lord Jesus will come "like a thief in the night" (1 Thess. 5:2). Ready or not, here he comes!

The Last Promises in the Bible

When Jesus comes, it will be everything we ever hoped for. All the ancient promises will come true—every last one of them: the promise of a golden city and a royal wedding, the promise of healing for the nations, the covenant promise that God will be with us forever. Everything lost in paradise will be regained. Everything wounded will be healed. Everything broken will be made whole.

Maybe the best place to see what the Dutch theologian Abraham Kuyper called "the perfect coming luster" of God's kingdom is in the Revelation of John.[1] In the Bible's last apocalypse, the beloved apostle shares his true vision of what the world will be like when the kingdom comes—what it will be like then, and also what it is like now, as the kingdom of God enters the kingdom of this world.

Part way through his mysterious book, John describes a war in heaven between the angels of God and the demons of the Devil. Satan loses that war and gets cast out of heaven—an event that Revelation describes as a kingdom victory: "Now the salvation and the power and the kingdom of our God and the authority of his Christ have come, for the accuser of our brothers has been thrown down" (Rev. 12:10).

Yet it is clear from how the story continues that this was not the last battle. When Satan was thrown down from heaven, he fell upon the earth "in great wrath" (Rev. 12:12). To this very day, he is doing his very worst to keep the kingdom from ever coming. When things are not the way they are supposed to be, when the kingdom *doesn't* come, this is mainly the Devil's doing.

In vivid detail, Revelation describes the terrible evils that Satan brings into the world. Even if we do not always understand the imagery, or agree about the symbolism, we can all see the Devil's mortal hatred of the kingdom of God. And we have all experienced it. There are so many things that go wrong in the world: poverty and slavery, warfare and bloodshed, oppression and abuse. So many things go wrong in our own lives, too: think of all the times that we do not get treated fairly, or find the happiness we hoped for, or love others the way we should. When things go wrong, we should remember that a mighty and relentless enemy is working against us.

That is not the whole story, however, because one day God's kingdom will come in all its power and glory. Jesus will come again, the Devil will be defeated, and everything wrong will be made right. Here is how John described it, in the Bible's last promises:

> Then I saw a new heaven and a new earth, for the first heaven and the first earth had passed away, and the sea was no more. And I saw the holy city, new Jerusalem, coming down out of heaven from God, prepared as a bride adorned for her husband. And I heard a loud voice from the throne saying, "Behold, the dwelling place of God is with man. He will dwell with them, and they will be his people, and God himself will be with them as their God. He will wipe away every tear from their eyes, and death shall be no more, neither shall there be mourning, nor crying, nor pain anymore, for the former things have passed away."
>
> And he who was seated on the throne said, "Behold, I am making all things new." (Rev. 21:1–5)

This is what John saw, and as he continued to look, he saw some of the things that God was making new. See if you can imagine the scene:

> Then the angel showed me the river of the water of life, bright as crystal, flowing from the throne of God and of the Lamb through the middle of the street of the city; also, on either side of the river, the tree of life with its twelve kinds of fruit, yielding its fruit each month. The leaves of the tree were for the healing of the nations. No longer will there be anything accursed, but the throne of God and of the Lamb will be in it, and his servants will worship him. They will see his face, and his name will be on their forehead. And night will be no more. They will need no light of lamp or sun, for the Lord God will be their light, and they will reign forever and ever. (Rev. 22:1–5)

Promises Kept

What I find extraordinary in John's vision is the way it pulls together so many themes and images that run all the way through Scripture. If the promises of God are like streams and rivers, then the end of Revelation is the vast ocean into which they all flow. Everything in the Bible comes together at the coming of the kingdom.

Revelation hearkens back to Genesis in order to show us creation recapitulated. The last two chapters of the Bible form an *inclusio* with the first two chapters. The end reminds us of the beginning, when God made the heavens and the earth. When the kingdom comes, it will be like déjà vu, because God will make a "new heavens and a new earth" (Isa. 65:17; 2 Pet. 3:13). Once again, he will put his people in a garden. And like the first garden, a river will run through it, watering the tree of life. When we get to the end of the Bible, we see paradise regained. The promise of the first creation is renewed, as our first home is brought to its final perfection.

The heavenly garden will also be a city—the city of New Jerusalem. Thus all the promises that God ever made about building a holy city will also come true. There will be a throne in that city, and on the throne, a king, fulfilling all the promises that God made to the house of David about an everlasting kingdom.

When the kingdom comes, there will be a royal wedding, which is another promise fulfilled. One day we will celebrate the match made in heaven between the people of God as a beautiful bride and Jesus Christ as the worthy groom. The Bible often describes our relationship with God as a romance between husband and wife. Sadly, we have often been unfaithful to him. But despite our spiritual adultery, the love of God perseveres, and so our love relationship with him will find its matrimonial satisfaction in the kingdom of God.

John also tells us that when the kingdom comes—and maybe this is the best part—God will be with us. This is the ancient promise of the everlasting covenant—the promise that God first made to Abraham. God will be with us to be our God. Thus the divine presence that Adam and Eve enjoyed in the garden, but lost, will be restored. Is any promise more precious than the promise that God will be with us forever? That sacred promise will be fulfilled when the kingdom comes and we see Jesus face to face.

The major themes, the dominant images, and the greatest promises of the Bible—including the ones that go all the way back to early Genesis—all come together at the end, in the last two chapters. The garden in the city, the wedding of the spotless bride, the promise of God's presence: it will all come true. When God says, "Behold, I am making all things new" (Rev. 21:5), he means exactly what he says. He will not create "all new things," but take what he has already made and perfect it.

At the center of it all will be Jesus himself, the Lamb of God, sitting on his eternal throne. John Milton beautifully expressed this hope in one of his prayers. With a deep longing to see Jesus Christ at the coming of his kingdom, he prayed:

> Thy kingdom is now at hand, and thou standing at the door. Come forth out of thy royal chambers, O Prince of all the kings of the earth! Put on the visible robes of Thy imperial majesty, take up that unlimited scepter which thy Almighty Father hath bequeathed thee; for now the voice of thy bride calls thee, and all creatures sigh to be renewed.[2]

Milton's prayer is not an idle wish. It is a sincere and hopeful desire, based upon the promises of God.

No More Pain

As a citizen of God's kingdom, I long to see our royal Prince on his great day! I sigh to be renewed. I also hope fervently to see an end to all our earthly trials. John writes about this as well. The book of Revelation does more than simply tell us what will be *in* the kingdom, when all God's promises are fulfilled; it also tells us what will be kept *out of* the kingdom. When the kingdom comes—when the old order of things passes away and God makes all things new—there will be no more death and no more pain.

The longer we live, and the more experience we have of death and pain, the more precious these promises become. Start with God's promise about our pain. What pain have you suffered, or else suffered with and for the people you love?

We think first of physical pain—the sufferings that afflict the body because of injury or disease. But the deeper pains are the wounds that touch the soul. As we reflect on our experiences, some memories are still painful to the touch: the relationship that ended, the rejection that crushed our spirit, the words that hurt deeper than anyone else could understand. Maybe you have felt the pain of discovering that you are not as good as you thought you were at something you desperately wanted to be good at, or of trying and failing to escape a destructive sin, or of ending up in a black depression that swallowed up all your joy. In this life, there is no end to the pains we suffer.

I tasted this firsthand as I watched my teenage daughter first struggle with a serious and life-changing illness. For several years, she had experienced low-grade pain in her joints. As the pain intensified, it became apparent that she had *ankylosing spondylitis*—a degenerative disease that in severe cases eventually causes a fusing of the spine. There is no cure—a fact that sprang out at me with awful malice when I first read it online.

As my daughter suffered various kinds of pain—fatigue, nausea, cyclical vomiting every night for weeks, days when it was difficult to walk even one block without tears coming to her eyes—I went through the pains a father bears for a suffering child. I fretted about her missing months and months of school. It grieved me to push her around in a wheelchair at the zoo. I worried about the future, not understanding how her diagnosis fit in with her long-term dream to educate underprivileged children overseas.

But I know this: my daughter has a heavenly Father who loves her infinitely more than I do—a Father who has a better plan. What is more, I believe that one day her pain will come to an end. I believe this because God has promised it: when the kingdom comes there will be no more pain!

No More Death

Nor will there be any death. This too is the promise of God, through the resurrection of Jesus Christ.

To put this promise into perspective, consider the testimony of Dr. Roger Lundin, who is the Arthur F. Holmes Professor of Faith and Learning at Wheaton College. When he talks about God's work in his life, Professor Lundin often describes the disturbing nightmares he had as a teenager in the weeks and months after his brother died. The two of them had shared a room together, with their beds on opposite walls. Lundin had a recurring dream that his beloved brother was in his usual place, except that life had passed from his mortal body. In the dream someone would tell him that if only he could reach out and touch the body, his brother would spring back to life and be restored to his family. But of course for one reason or another he would always fail to make any life-giving connection with his brother. So he would wake up in a cold sweat, feeling guilty for his failure. Then he would look over at the empty bed and experience the empty desolation of his loss all over again.

As I consider Dr. Lundin's story, I can't help but think of the extraordinary story that Luke tells about the time when Jesus reached out and touched a dead man's bed (Luke 7:11–17). The Savior was traveling to a town called Nain, and as he came near the gates, he met a funeral procession. A widow's only young son had died, and the whole town had gathered to carry his body out for burial. But when Jesus reached out to touch the dead man's bed, death itself was stopped in its tracks. A single touch, one word of command, and the dead man came back to life!

Jesus Christ has authority over life and death. By the power of his resurrection, he will never die again. And by that same power, he will raise every one of his followers to eternal life. We claim this promise for every believer in Christ who has gone ahead of us into the grave, and then on to glory. We claim it for parents and grandparents, brothers and sisters, family and friends. We claim it for all the beloved people we have lost and hope to see again.

Whether it comes by disease or misadventure, or simply by the effects of old age, death is our last enemy. But when the kingdom comes, death itself will be defeated. Jesus was only the first to rise. His plan is for all his children to rise, and never to die again. Therefore, at the coming of Christ, everyone who belongs to Christ will be made alive. "Then comes the end," the Scripture says, "when he delivers the kingdom to God the Father" (1 Cor. 15:24). And when Jesus delivers the kingdom to the Father—the Bible is explicit about this—that will be the end of death. "For he must reign until he has put all his enemies under his feet," and "the last enemy to be destroyed is death" (vv. 25–26).

Witnesses for the Kingdom

The more we know about the kingdom of God, and the more we meditate on its coming, the more obvious it becomes that the kingdom is not something we can bring into the world. In this suffering world, we will never see an end to pain. We do not have the power to raise life out of death, or to regain the paradise that we have lost, or to fulfill any of the other ancient promises of God. These powers belong only to the Savior who has conquered sin and death through the cross and the empty tomb. Therefore, the kingdom is something that Jesus brings— only Jesus.

There is something we can do, however, and that is bear witness to the kingdom. The people who believe that God is planning to make a whole new creation are the same people who work for that world now, doing everything they can to set things right. By our words of gospel truth and our deeds of Christian love, we testify to the reality of kingdom come. What we do for Jesus reflects the values of his kingdom and thus gives evidence of our surprising hope in a whole new creation. It also creates a context in which it is credible for people to believe our gospel. How will people ever believe in the kingdom of God if they do not see us live in the joyful anticipation of its coming?

There are thousands of ways for us to show that we believe in the kingdom of God. We do it by persevering through pain and continuing to praise God. We do it by making art that is true to the possibility of redemption. We do it by giving our time to fatherless children. We do it by putting other people first in all the little things of life, the way that Jesus would. We do it by saving the unborn, healing the sick, feeding the poor, releasing the oppressed, and serving the elderly. In short, we demonstrate our faith in the kingdom to come by responding with love and mercy wherever things are ugly, unjust, or inconsistent with the redemptive purposes of God. When we respond this way, we are not just making this world a better place. We are doing something much more important: we are showing this world what the next world will be.

The philosopher Nicholas Wolterstorff uses Old Testament vocabulary to describe our kingdom activities. He calls them "the work of shalom." Wolterstorff writes:

> Shalom is both God's cause in the world and our human calling. Even though the full incursion of shalom into our history will be divine gift and not merely human achievement, even though its episodic incursion into our lives now also has a dimension of divine gift, nonetheless it is shalom that we are to work and struggle for. We are not to stand around, hands folded, waiting for shalom to arrive. We are workers in God's cause, his peace-workers.[3]

When we do this work—when we signify on earth what the kingdom will be in heaven—it becomes more plausible for people to believe in kingdom come. By the work of the Holy Spirit, people who see us live in the hope of the kingdom come will be ready to believe the good news that Christ is King.

A simple example of kingdom witness comes from the ministry of Samaritan's Purse. One year to the day after a massive earthquake, tsunami, and nuclear accident devastated Japan, Franklin Graham held an evangelistic rally in the city of Sendai. Services were held in a sports complex that had served as a temporary morgue in the days following the country's triple disaster. During the rally, hundreds of Japanese found new life in Jesus Christ. One family said that they had come for one reason: after the tragedy they had suffered, many people came to help, but only the Christians were still there a year later, doing kingdom work. They were clearing debris, rebuilding homes, providing food and clothing, counseling souls in distress—all in the name of Jesus. The service of those believers in Christ made it credible for a family to believe in a Savior they had never seen and thus to come into his kingdom.

Wherever we go, all of us are called to this kind of witness. Our goal individually as Christians and corporately as the body of Christ is to give people good reason to believe in kingdom come. By the joy of our worship, the truth of our words, the integrity of our faith, the beauty of our art, the purity of our justice, and the tenderness of our compassion, we want people to believe that there really is a Savior who will make everything right in the end—when the kingdom comes.

When Gene Schmidt traveled to Philadelphia to perform a work of art entitled *Lovetown PA*, he took with him the entire text of 1 Corinthians 13. The artist had cut each character of the biblical text into a separate piece of wood, one foot square, forming a stencil. He then put the words of 1 Corinthians 13 on public display in neighborhoods across the city. In front of one building the text read, "Now we see in a glass darkly, but then . . ."

"Then *what?*" asked a curious bystander.

"Then face to face," Schmidt said, to which the stranger responded, "I can hardly wait!"

At the end of Revelation, the apostle John said that his words, which are "trustworthy and true," prophesy events that "must soon take place" (Rev. 22:6). Then he quoted the last words of Christ that are recorded in Scripture, "Surely I am coming soon." And when he heard these words, John cried out, "Amen. Come, Lord Jesus!" (v. 20).

This is our prayer as well: Come, Lord Jesus! And when we make this our prayer, we stand under the benediction that John pronounced on everyone who lives for Christ and his kingdom: "The grace of the Lord Jesus be with all. Amen" (Rev. 22:21).

Notes

Chapter 1: The Kingdom Is Near

1. Laurie Essig, "No Rapture, but the End Days Are upon Us," *The Chronicle of Higher Education* (May 24, 2011).

2. Michael J. Kruger explores the drama of this moment in "The Return of the King: Exploring the Kingdom of God in Jesus' Inaugural Sermon," *Modern Reformation* (January/February, 2011), 25.

3. Christoph Schwobel in *The End of the World and the Ends of God*, ed. J. C. Polkinghorne and M. Welker (Trinity Press International, 2000), 111.

4. Graeme Goldsworthy, *Gospel and Kingdom: A Christian Interpretation of the Old Testament*, Biblical Classics Library (Carlisle, Cumbria: Paternoster, 1994), 51.

5. James Davison Hunter, *To Change the World: The Irony, Tragedy, and Possibility of Christianity in the Late Modern World* (Oxford: Oxford University Press, 2010), 234.

6. The full and tragic story of Jan van Leiden is recounted by Jonathan Kirsch in *A History of the End of the World: How the Most Controversial Book in the Bible Changed the Course of Western Civilization* (San Francisco: Harper, 2006), 165–66.

7. Hal Lindsay with C. C. Carlson, *The Late Great Planet Earth* (Grand Rapids, MI: Zondervan, 1970).

8. Edgar Whisenant, *88 Reasons Why the Rapture Will Be in 1988* (Nashville, TN: World Bible Society, 1988).

9. Cyril of Alexandria, "Commentary on Luke," in *Luke*, ed. Ar-

thur A. Just Jr., Ancient Christian Commentary on Scripture, NT 3 (Downers Grove, IL: InterVarsity, 2003), 271.

Chapter 2: Mine Is the Kingdom

1. Mark Buchanan, "The Cult of the Next Thing," *Christianity Today* (September 6, 1999), http://www.ctlibrary.com/ct/1999/September6/9ta062.html.
2. Mat Honan, "Fever Dream of a Guilt Ridden Gadget Reporter," *Gizmodo*, January 11, 2012.
3. Piers Morgan, in an interview with Joel Osteen on CNN's *Piers Morgan Tonight*, October 4, 2011.
4. Buchanan, "Trapped in the Cult of the Next Thing."
5. Wendell Berry, interviewed in *Modern Reformation* (November/December 2001): 40.
6. John Wesley, *The Methodist Service Book* (London: Methodist Publishing House, 1975), D10.

Chapter 3: Thy Kingdom Come

1. Frank Darabont, *The Shawshank Redemption: The Shooting Script* (New York: Newmarket Press, 1996), 61–62.
2. James Davison Hunter, *To Change the World: The Irony, Tragedy, and Possibility of Christianity in the Late Modern World* (Oxford: Oxford University Press, 2010), 233.
3. *The Valley of Vision: A Collection of Puritan Prayers and Devotions*, ed. Arthur Bennett, rev. ed. (Edinburgh: Banner of Truth, 2002), 138.
4. John Bunyan, *The Pilgrim's Progress* (New York: Penguin Books, 2002), 134.
5. Spiros Zodhiates, *The Lord's Prayer*, rev. ed. (Chattanooga, TN: AMG, 1991), 141.
6. This story is related in E. M. Bounds, *The Purpose in Prayer* (Grand Rapids: Christian Classics Ethereal Library, 2001), 53.
7. F. B. Meyer, *Elijah* (Fort Washington, PA: Christian Literature Crusade, 1992), 87.
8. Edith Schaeffer, *L'Abri* (Wheaton, IL: Tyndale, 1969), 92.
9. Ibid., 97.

Chapter 4: The Forever Kingdom

1. John Polkinghorne, *The God of Hope and the End of the World* (New Haven, CT: Yale University Press, 2002), 6–11.
2. See Raymond E. Brown, *The Birth of the Messiah: A Commentary on the Infancy Narratives in the Gospels of Matthew and Luke*, rev. ed., Anchor Bible Reference Library (New York: Doubleday, 1993), 358–60.
3. Timothy Dudley-Smith, *Tell Out My Soul*, 1961.
4. Martyn Lloyd-Jones, "Bringing Down the Mighty," reprinted in *Evangelicals Now* (December 1998): 13.
5. John Donne, quoted in Polkinghorne, 98.

Chapter 5: Missing the Kingdom

1. *Sanhedrin*, 10.1.
2. Cyril of Alexandria, "Commentary on Luke," in *Luke*, ed. Arthur A. Just Jr., Ancient Christian Commentary on Scripture, NT 3 (Downers Grove, IL: InterVarsity, 2003), 299.
3. Chad Allen, interview televised on CNN's *Larry King Live!*, January 2006.
4. Cecil Frances Alexander, "There Is a Green Hill Far Away," 1848.
5. C. S. Lewis, *The Magician's Nephew* (London: Bodley Head, 1955), 155–58.
6. Thomas Boston, *The Complete Works of the Late Rev. Thomas Boston of Ettrick*, ed. Samuel M'Millan, 12 vols. (London, 1853; repr. Wheaton, IL: Richard Owen Roberts, 1980), 8:244.
7. Billy Graham, "The Time Is Short," *Wheaton* (November 1976): 3.
8. David Gooding, *According to Luke: A New Exposition of the Third Gospel* (Grand Rapids, MI: Eerdmans, 1987), 262.

Chapter 6: Proclaiming the Kingdom

1. The story of Vedran Smajlovic is recounted by Stephen Nichols in *Welcome to the Story: Reading, Loving, and Living God's Word* (Wheaton, IL: Crossway, 2011), 88–89.
2. Eric Liddell, quoted in Joel S. Woodruff, "Eric Liddell: Muscular Disciple and Olympic Champion," *Knowing and Doing* (Summer 2012): 19.

3. Herman Ridderbos, *The Coming of the Kingdom* (Phillipsburg, NJ: P&R, 1962), 149.

4. David A. Horner, *Mind Your Faith: A Student's Guide to Thinking and Living Well* (Downers Grove, IL: InterVarsity, 2011), 103.

5. Charles Spurgeon, "Metropolitan Tabernacle Statistics," *Sword and Trowel* (April 1865): n.p.

6. Leith Anderson's remarks are quoted by Jerry Root in "When All the World Hears," *Decision* (November 2011): 29.

7. This story is recounted by Charles Spurgeon in *Metropolitan Tabernacle Pulpit* (July 31, 1864), 450.

Chapter 7: When the Kingdom Doesn't Come

1. Michael Wilcock, *The Message of Luke*, The Bible Speaks Today (Downers Grove, IL: InterVarsity, 1979), 174.

2. J. C. Ryle, *Expository Thoughts on the Gospels, Luke* (1858; repr. Cambridge, UK: James Clarke, 1976), 2:306.

3. William Carey, quoted in "The Lessons of Jabez," *Christianity Today* (March 2006), 27.

4. Rachel Lamb, from a Wheaton College Chapel testimony, Spring 2012. Used with permission.

Chapter 8: When the Kingdom Comes

1. Abraham Kuyper, *Calvinism: Six Stone Foundation Lectures* (Grand Rapids, MI: Eerdmans, 1943), 165–66.

2. John Milton, *Animadversions upon the Remonstrants Defence against Smectymnuus* (London: Thomas Underhill, 1641), 493.

3. Nicholas Wolterstorff, *Until Justice and Peace Embrace: The Kuyper Lectures for 1981 Delivered at the Free University of Amsterdam* (Grand Rapids, MI: Eerdmans, 1983), 72.

General Index

Scripture Index

Celebrating the Transforming Power of Grace

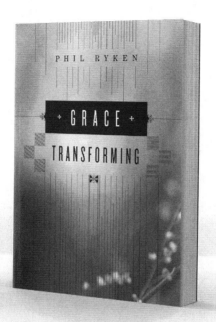

"I so appreciate Ryken's extraordinary insights. . . . If you are seeking a fresh look at your Lord and your own desperate need of him, this is the book for you!"

JONI EARECKSON TADA, Founder and CEO, Joni and Friends International Disability Center

"In a culture of high expectation, Ryken teaches that grace is not only greater than all our sin, it is also release from human pressures and fuel for fruitful joy."

BRYAN CHAPELL, Senior Pastor, Grace Presbyterian Church (PCA), Peoria, Illinois

---

For more information, visit crossway.org.